CONVERSATIONS ON
WHEN EVERYTHING IS MISSIONS
REDISCOVERING THE MISSION OF THE CHURCH

EDITED BY
DENNY SPITTERS &
MATTHEW ELLISON

Conversations on When Everything Is Missions: Rediscovering the Mission of the Church

edited by Denny Spitters & Matthew Ellison

copyright ©2020 Pioneers-USA & Sixteen:Fifteen

ISBN: 978-0-9852192-7-7

Contents

Foreword

by Denny Spitters & Matthew Ellison

In December of 2017 we published *When Everything Is Missions* (WEIM). This labor of love flowed from our experience, convictions and passion for the priority of the gospel and its advancement to all nations, tribes and tongues. We stated, "Churches don't do missions well—because they do not think about missions well."[1]

In our combined 75 years of experience, we have seen a significant shift in how *missions* is defined and carried out by churches. Rather than a focus on our responsibility to "go therefore and make disciples of all nations," we see a North American church and its leaders focused on "redefining" and "rethinking" missions in a way that replaces gospel advancement with personal, social and humanistic preferences and agendas.

Prior to our first print run, we sent our original manuscript to some 75 trusted church leaders, friends and mentors whom we love and respect. We asked them to read the manuscript and give critical feedback to help us be true and accurate to the Word of God and sound in our missiology (the theology of missions). We benefited from many positive and critical responses and are indebted to all of them for their feedback.

One objection we heard was that our book lacked empirical evidence proving the decline of missions and the gospel in the church. Without objective research, our observations might not be worthy of much consideration.

WHAT WE'VE SEEN

Admittedly, our conclusions did not come from a scientific research survey, but primarily from our missions experience with churches, our combined examination of evangelical missions historically and our observance of the present-day Church through the lens of both healthy biblical discipleship and Jesus' five foundational New Testament commissioning statements for missions. To our view, more churches have wandered off the path of those five foundational imperatives than have remained on a "true north" course of pursuit.

One of the greatest barriers for the advancement of missions in our churches has been the consistent negative analysis of past missionary efforts under the guise of rethinking and reimagining missions. Have missionaries made mistakes in the modern missions movements of the past 150 years? Of course! Are we not all fallible? Yet this "rethinking" has led many church leaders into a passivity and apathy bordering on *immobilization* as significant gospel advancement of the past 100 years is brought into critical disrepute.

The schema often used is to build upon anecdotal past negative missionary stories or appeal to strawmen and then pit the Great Commandment against the Great Commission. This has resulted in an increasingly suspect and pessimistic view of missions by younger generations in the church while evangelism and church planting are abandoned for causes of political and social justice. Consequently, the idea of taking the gospel where it is unknown by making disciples of all nations has become a scandalous thought to increasing numbers in the evangelical Church.

One thing is certain: The history of the last 200 years of modern missions is tied to the rise and decline of obedience and fidelity to the Word of God and Christ's Great Commission. Is what David Hesselgrave called the "Edinburgh Error" repeating itself?[2] We believe it is.

6

WHERE IS THE PROOF?

Little did we know that, during our writing of *WEIM*, a study had been commissioned by the Barna Group in partnership with the Seed Company called *Translating the Great Commission: What Spreading the Gospel Means to U.S. Christians in the 21st Century*. This research documented and validated what we had observed and experienced, revealing:

- "Half of all U.S. churchgoers (51 percent) say they are unfamiliar with the term 'the Great Commission.'"
- "If presented with a list of potential verses, just 37 percent recognize the correct passage that goes by this name."
- "Skepticism about the intent of missions and the Bible is high among U.S. adults, especially non-Christians. Some within the church, especially Millennials and ethnic minorities, are also wary of missions being misused."
- "Only 17 percent of Generation X and just 10 percent of Millennials say they know of the Bible text called the Great Commission (the final words of Jesus)!"[3]

What does all this mean? Why is there such great confusion about missions and the Great Commission?

Just as the Protestant Reformation was not focused on redefining the biblical gospel but rediscovering it, our answers will not be found in redefining missions but in rediscovering what is made clear about missions in God's Word. Knowing comes before doing, and it shapes and informs our doing.

WHY WE WROTE THIS BOOK

We designed this book as a companion to *When Everything Is Missions* for the purpose of helping you think about what missions can be and should be. It is written by an array of people who have wrestled with the effects of what we might call "the Great Confusion" and who will help guide us to think well about missions (the knowing) so that our engagement (the doing) in missions will be shaped by sound biblical understanding. You'll find church leaders, pastors, congregants, missiologists, missions agency leaders, mobilizers, seminary professors and missionaries who are astute, discerning and passionate about knowing before doing. We are grateful for their effort, energy and time given as an offering from the best of their wisdom, experience and training.

Get ready to be challenged, provoked and encouraged to grow into God's vision for His glory among all nations, tribes and tongues!

As you read, we hope you will come to understand the eternal significance and crucial imperative of the words of Jesus:

"All authority in heaven and on earth has been given to me. Go therefore and make disciples of all nations, baptizing them in the name of the Father and of the Son and of the Holy Spirit, teaching them to observe all that I have commanded you. And behold, I am with you always, to the end of the age" (Matthew 28:18-20).

May we all have ears to hear from J. Hudson Taylor, a profound disciple and 19th-century missionary to China who said: "The Great Commission is not an option to be considered; it is a command to be obeyed."

Denny Spitters, Vice President of Church Partnerships for Pioneers USA, has served in many church staff roles as worship, missions and small group pastor and understands the significance of the local church. Denny served on the staff of two megachurches, directed a parachurch ministry and helped plant several churches. He also spent 15 years as a business owner.

Matthew Ellison served as a missions pastor at a megachurch for nine years. During this time, he realized a growing wave of churches were no longer content to only support missions. Instead they desired active global engagement. This led to the founding of Sixteen:Fifteen, where he serves as President and Church Missions Coach. Since 2004 he has been coaching churches across the United States, helping them to develop missions vision and strategy.

Part I:
How Did We Get Here?

"Ponder the path of your feet; then all your ways will be sure." — Proverbs 4:26

"How we define mission today determines to a great degree how we'll do missions today and tomorrow."
— Ed Stetzer[4]

chapter 1

Currents of Change: How Did Everything Become Missions?[5]

by J. D. Payne

The Church has reached a point in history at which missions means anything she does in the world. Missions is multifaceted. The Church has medical missions, relief missions, short-term missions (which includes a multitude of activities), missions to the elderly, orphan-care missions, church-planting missions, leadership development and educational missions, evangelistic missions, disaster-relief missions and construction missions, just to mention a few examples. Missionaries can be teachers, church planters, farmers, seminary professors and engineers. We now live in a time when the Church thinks of itself as doing missions even if the gospel is never shared.

My assigned task is to attempt to answer the question: How did the Church get to this point? Everything did not become missions overnight. Our present reality has been a long journey. There is no single source that is the cause of such diversity. Rather, just as several tributaries flow together to create a river, there are at least five currents that brought us to the present situation.

CURRENT #1: PROBLEM OF LANGUAGE

While biblical concepts have been assigned to words such as *mission, missions* and *missionary,* these are extrabiblical terms. Such words are not found in Hebrew or Greek but derive from Latin. The earliest use has been connected to the Jesuits.

We now live at a time when the Church thinks of itself as doing missions even if the gospel is never shared.

André Seumois notes that Ignatius of Loyola was using variations of *missions* in 1540.[6] The language of *mission* and *missions* is used in Ignatius' *The Constitutions of the Society of Jesus,* which was first approved by the first General Congregation in 1558, with such terminology referring to being sent into the world "for the greater glory of God and the good of souls, whether among the faithful or unbelievers."[7] While God's glory may have been part of the motivation behind such kingdom endeavors, a great deal of Catholic missionary activities became closely connected with European military and colonial expansion. Christianization and civilization were often two goals of both church and state. The sacred and secular often had an intimate union.

Whenever the Church lacks exegetical support for her theology, extrabiblical nomenclature can result in concepts with a variety of meanings. Church culture and context become most important as a defining factor of mission. Given this relativistic understanding, David Bosch was correct when he noted in *Transforming Mission* that "mission remains undefinable; it should never be incarcerated in the narrow confines of our own predilections. The most we can hope for is to formulate some *approximations* of what mission is all about."[8] Years later, Michael W. Stroope described mission as a "broad river in which there is space for many usages and meanings" and a term "quite elastic in its meaning."[9] Such fluidity exists partially due to meaning and activity being socially constructed in the moment (or across an epoch).

The Latin (*mitto*) origin of *mission, missions* and *missionary* is not sufficient for the development of a proper biblical understanding of the Great Commission activities of the Church. Andreas J. Köstenberger was correct when he wrote, "Any understanding of a biblical theology of mission must derive its contours from the biblical material itself rather than being submerged by extrabiblical definitions."[10] But what if *mission* is not found in the Bible?

While such terminology is common parlance and near and dear to our hearts, it has been part of the process that has resulted in everything becoming missions. If there is no biblical word for *mission, missions, or missionary,* who is to say that my definition is more accurate than yours?[11]

CURRENT #2: THEOLOGICAL SHIFTS

Theological shifts in the 18th through 20th centuries moved the Church away from historic orthodox teachings regarding inspiration, theology proper, Christology and personal and cosmic eschatology, just to name a few areas. The Bible was subjected to critical study with an anti-supernatural bias. Ethical monotheism was viewed as the result of societal evolution. Jesus became an example to follow, while the significance of His penal-substitutionary atonement and honor/shame removal act was relegated to the dustbin. Sin, judgement and hell were seen as psychological burdens and to be discarded as quickly as possible. The academy had created some of the greatest heretics who remained cloaked in ecclesial culture and language.

For some, humanity became the center of mission.

During this period, pluralism and inclusivism were growing in influence. For some, humanity became the center of mission. The Church, Jesus and God existed for the improvement of society. Missionary activities were to improve quality of life but should "never violate the sanctity of human personality."[12] Religions became equals.

The publication of William Ernest Hocking's *Re-Thinking Missions* revealed how humanism and liberal theology influenced missionary thought and practice in certain circles:

> "If the conception of hell changes, if attention is drawn away from the fear of God's punitive justice in everlasting torment of the unsaved, to happier conceptions of destiny, if there is a shift of concern from other worldly issues to the problems of sin and suffering in the present life, these changes will immediately alter that view of the perils of the soul which gave to the original motive of Protestant missions much of its poignant urgency. Generally speaking, these changes have occurred."[13]

While many mission leaders spoke against liberal and neo-orthodox theologies, over time, aspects of such theological systems began to trickle down from the academy and influenced local churches and mission agencies. Conversionistic missiology and the exclusivity of Christ were sometimes avoided for more palatable practices that encouraged more people to go, believing it were possible to witness through presence alone.

CURRENT #3: VALUE OF INSTANT GRATIFICATION

The western drive for quick results emerged from a value system that facilitated immediate and quantifiable accomplishments. A roof could be added to a church's building faster than a church could be planted among an unreached people. Antibiotics could be distributed much easier than the gospel could be shared in a different language.

A roof could be added to a church's building faster than a church could be planted among an unreached people.

In his research on short-term missions, Edwin Zehner notes that by the early 21st century, immediate gratification was a growing value among evangelicals: "Yet overall by 2007, especially in North America, there had been a subtle shift to new rhetoric and expectations, including greater interest in practical action and more realistic notions of what short-term offerings can accomplish."[14] If teams (short- or long-term) could do good activities in the name of Jesus and experience quick results, then why not develop and give more attention to methods and strategies to support such actions?

CURRENT #4: EVANGELISM AND SOCIAL JUSTICE DEBATE

The evangelism and social justice debate had a long history in the 20th and 21st centuries. The tension was felt even as recently as Lausanne III in Cape Town (2010) when during a plenary session, John Piper asked, "Could Lausanne say? Could the evangelical Church say, 'For Christ's sake, we Christians care about all suffering, especially eternal suffering'?"[15]

The world has always been filled with areas of significant physical and spiritual need. Evangelicals have always been moved with the desire to take bandages and the gospel to the world. Such is the right way of the kingdom citizen.

However, faced with such global needs, the Church in the West does not naturally gravitate toward gospel proclamation, but drifts away from it and toward care for suffering. Our eyes and hearts are often more in tune with the immediate than the eternal. The Church must work diligently to be intentional about disciple making.

Our eyes and hearts are often more in tune with the immediate than the eternal.

John Stott was a leader in the area of global evangelization and also championed the Church's responsibility of social justice. However, the language used in a section of his influential book *Christian Mission in the Modern World* creates an opportunity for the Church to neglect gospel proclamation due to the ubiquitous realities of suffering and social injustices. He writes:

"To see need and to possess the remedy compels love to act, and whether the action will be evangelistic or social, or indeed political, depends on what we 'see' and what we 'have.'

"This does not mean that words and works, evangelism and social action, are such inseparable partners that all of us must engage in both all the time. Situations vary, and so do Christian callings. As for situations, there will be times when a person's eternal destiny is the most urgent consideration, for we must not forget that men without Christ are perishing. But there will certainly be other times when a person's material need is so pressing that he would not be able to hear the gospel if we shared it with him... If our enemy is hungry, our biblical mandate is not to evangelize him but to feed him (Romans 12:20)!"[16]

Such language communicates there are *times* when eternal matters are not ultimate. In his noble attempt to draw attention to the truth that the pain of suffering can rightly hinder one from hearing the gospel, he opens a door for missions to avoid identifying with proclamation. I cannot help but think many people have taken such words and thoughts to an unhealthy direction—one not intended by Stott. Instead of the Church expecting the "other times" as *exceptional* when urgent relief is necessary to save a life, she has come to view these times as expected, the norm, and has adjusted her mission strategy and methods to support a multitude of activities at the expense of disciple making.

The Church is able to travel faster and farther than any generation.

CURRENT #5: GOOD INTENTIONS + TECHNOLOGICAL ADVANCEMENTS

Christians are called to maximize their talents, gifts, abilities and skills for the glory of God. It is natural for the Church to leverage such blessings at home. However, the world is our parish. Kingdom citizens began to recognize that any good they could do at home is something that should be done abroad. Communication developments, diminished costs and speed of international travel and the safety of spending time in other countries resulted in large numbers of western Christians going to serve the nations.

The Church in the West recognized intercultural engagement could become the practice of the many and not something exclusively for the few. By 2005, 1.6 million US adult church members were participating in international short-term mission trips.[17] While many short-term teams do participate in evangelistic and church-planting endeavors, a growing number go to serve in other areas. A. Scott Moreau found that a larger percentage of short-term workers sent by US agencies from 2001-2005 chose to participate in relief/development and education/training rather than primary activities of evangelism and discipleship.[18]

Without neglecting Her Holy-Spirit-designed diversity, the Church must articulate the uniqueness of her apostolic work in both biblical terms and understanding as she labors to make disciples of all peoples.

The Church is able to travel faster and farther than in any previous generation. She is able to engage in a large amount of disciple making and service in the name of Christ. Yet the thought remains that whatever the Church does at home is considered evangelism or ministry and whatever is done "overseas" is considered missions. The regularity and quantity of Christians going into the world to do kingdom activities helped develop the understanding that all such international work is missionary activity.

CONCLUSION

Missions has come to mean a multitude of things to different people. This unclear understanding of the term (including its derivatives) and concept developed over time as several currents of thought and practice converged. Kingdom citizens should glorify God by serving the nations with differing skills and advocating for social justice issues. The Church needs more people to go! Wise stewards work with urgency and desire to know what is working to bring about kingdom results; life is a vapor (James 4:14), and the Day approaches.

Clarity and distinction are needed. He gave "some" not *all* to be... (Ephesians 4:11-12). An identifiable difference clearly existed in Acts 6:1-7. There are a variety of service and activities (1 Corinthians 12:5-6). Without neglecting her Spirit-designed diversity, the Church must articulate the uniqueness of her apostolic work in both biblical terms and understanding as she labors to make disciples of all peoples.

J. D. Payne serves as an Associate Professor of Christian Ministry at Samford University. He has published 13 books on missions and evangelism, hosts a podcast (Strike the Match) and writes frequently at jdpayne.org.

chapter 2

Deconstructing the Great Commission

by Dr. Ted Esler

INTRODUCTION

I like to say missiology is a dark science. So much of the missiological reflection that we can read today is critiquing missions and very little of it is positive. Unlike the many armchair theologians and missions experts (like me, by the way), missionaries are people who must *do* something. They cannot simply talk about missions. They act on the Great Commission. They share the gospel of Jesus Christ. In doing so they attempt to turn the concepts and ideas of the Bible into understandable, contextually sound arguments and persuade others about the truthfulness of those ideas.

Missionaries should be open to critique, of course. There is no doubt that colonial models of mission, patronizing approaches to relationships, cultural insensitivity and so on have hurt the advance of the gospel. Yet, the criticism of the missionary enterprise has created a paralyzing, antagonist view of missions in the churches of the US and Canada. It has created a warped view of both the historical missionary movement and contemporary missions in the minds of some. Rather than contributing positively to the advance of the kingdom, it may be hindering our understanding of what is happening globally.

TAKING APART THE GREAT COMMISSION

Deconstructionism is a literary and philosophical term that emerged in the 1960s. Originally, it was the questioning of traditional assumptions regarding how we understand terminology. This school of philosophy says that words in sentences are abstract representations of the ideas they represent. Pulling apart those abstract meanings destroy the "face value" those words were attempting to communicate. I am using the term more broadly than this.

Today there is an almost constant call for a re-envisioning of missions.

An illustration may serve to highlight this. I recently saw an internet meme that made me laugh and cry at the same time. It was a traditional image of Jesus telling the disciples to feed the 5,000. Jesus is standing with His arms extended, explaining to the disciples that they were now to feed these people. A couple of disciples looked up lovingly (but concerned) and a huge crowd was in the background. The top of the image had a line of text that read, "You want us to feed these people?" The bottom of the image said, "But that would create dependency!" Can feeding people create dependency? Of course, it can. Does that mean that Jesus was erring by feeding people? I think not.

Today there is an almost constant call for a re-envisioning of missions. Authors like Dyrness and Engel[19], Scott Bessenecker[20] and Michael Stroope[21] have written books critical of contemporary mission. These three books critique missionary agencies, missionary structure and the use of the term "mission" in any way. Richard Stearns[22] similarly called for a reframing of how we understand the message of Christ and how we share it both locally and globally.

Missions pastors of large churches tend to view missionaries as ineffective and believe that traditional missionaries need a significant overhaul in their approach.

My personal experience suggests that nowhere is there more frustration about missionary efforts than among the megachurch missions pastors across North America. The critique from this group is decidedly different than the authors previously mentioned. Missions pastors of large churches tend to view missionaries as ineffective and believe that traditional missionaries need a significant overhaul in their approach. A quick internet search of the two words "rethinking" and "missions" turns up pages and pages of content. Much of that material is driven by a restlessness about how the Great Commission is (or isn't) being expressed by the Church. Deconstructionism relays the message that the Great Commission, as it is expressed in the contemporary Church (including missionary agencies and similar organized efforts), is theologically and historically suspect.

PUTTING HUMPTY DUMPTY BACK TOGETHER AGAIN

The amazing thing to me about these critiques is that we live in an era where global Church growth has been explosive. Missionaries have had *at least some part* in this growth if not the greatest. The Church outside the West has multiplied many times over while the Western Church (the source of most of the critique) fights for relevance in its own culture.

Imagine counting Christians in 1910 during the landmark Edinburgh Missionary Conference. Ninety percent of all known believers lived in Western lands. Today, the script is almost flipped. The modern missionary movement has penetrated more than half of the world's people groups. One might argue that this has happened despite the missionary. One often cited example is the mainland Chinese Church. The trope goes that it was not until missionaries left that the Church began to grow. These critics will have to answer to the many martyrs, mostly European, who gave their lives to plant the seed that remained.

Consider that the missionary movement the West spawned is spilling over into the rest of the world. When we read of growing missionary movements in Asia, South America and Africa, we should recognize that these are the fruits of what has gone before. Is this simply more Western exploitation and cultural imperialism? I suppose to find that out you would need to sit with an African missionary, as I did a few months ago, and learn of his heart for lost Muslims, what his missionary service has cost him and how he intends to spend the balance of his life. At no point did he lament the presence of white Europeans in his tribal land or of overly eager North American missionaries today.

Should we be happy with the status quo? Certainly not. Are there missionaries who act inappropriately and do things which bring disrepute to the name of Christ? Of course, they are people after all. Yet we should also recognize that the fragile human systems we have created have yielded a harvest. Perhaps the call to throw the baby out with the bathwater should be somewhat muted.

RETHINKING RETHINKING

In 1932, *The Laymen's Foreign Missions Inquiry* was launched by such luminaries as John D. Rockefeller and John Mott.

While Rockefeller is known for his wealth, Mott was an influential voice in a previous generation's missionary efforts. Well financed and executed via three teams of researchers sent out to four Asian countries, a book was written about their findings and published in 1932. The title? *Re-Thinking Missions.* How ironic that they were rethinking missions long before our current rethinking.

What started out as an assessment of missionary work turned into a redefining of the missionary task itself that ultimately led to its demise.

The Laymen's Foreign Missions Inquiry turned out to be more than an evaluation of missionary work. It was a deconstruction of the missionary paradigm, not unlike contemporary efforts. The report introduced a generation of mainline denominations to the concept that missionary work should be primarily concerned with social justice and not the salvation of the lost. In the ensuing years, many mainline churches adopted this view of missions and consequently stopped doing mission altogether. What started out as an assessment of missionary work turned into a redefining of the missionary task itself that ultimately led to its demise.

Today, mainline missionary efforts are mostly found in the non-Western branches of these denominations. They see their role as re-evangelizing their Western counterparts. Could it be that in our current age of deconstruction we too will lose the basics of the Great Commission as these forebearers did?

The Great Commission is not the same as Great Commandment. Can these two, the Great Commandment and Great Commission, be separated from one another? This has been the unproductive argument of the past century. Let us agree

25

that they cannot be separated. However, the Great Commission usually falls victim to being "eaten" by the Great Commandment and loses its primary attributes (going, discipling the nations, teaching them to obey all and baptizing). Feeding the poor, taking care of widows, fighting injustice and many other important biblical concepts are simply broader than the Great Commission. When missionary work has been torn asunder by critics, these broader themes are often put forward under the guise of a new definition of mission. As Steve Addison has noted in his new book *The Rise and Fall of Movements*:

> "A shift has taken place over the last century in the Western understanding of God's mission and the part we play in it. That shift has resulted in what I call the 'missional fog' surrounding Western churches. Increasingly 'mission' is framed in political and social terms—fighting for economic justice and world peace, saving the planet, overcoming patriarchy and gender inequality, establishing kingdom businesses and growing organic vegetables. All these activities and causes have been classified as 'mission.' But these are not the core missionary task."[23]

CONCLUSION

I myself have deconstructed the missionary efforts of others. Not long ago I wrote an article about business as missions becoming the new colonialism (consider that we are sending out businessman just like the British Empire did some hundreds of years ago). It is helpful to reflect and consider the ramifications of our actions and deeds. However, we should also carefully consider the ramifications of our critiques.

As a young missionary working cross-culturally, I once criticized the small indigenous church present in the culture in which I worked. My mentor, a wiser, older missionary, asked me, "Ted, how would you feel if I criticized your wife?" I looked at him with a quizzical look on my face. Then he reminded me that I was criticizing the bride of Christ.

This brought a much-needed humility to my evaluation. This is perhaps the most important step we can take as we pass judgment on others.

Does the Great Commission really need to be rethought? Perhaps better, it needs rediscovery by a new generation.

Does the Great Commission really need to be rethought? Perhaps better, it needs rediscovery by a new generation. Perhaps it needs new expression in a new culture or era. Yet, the basic command of Christ to make disciples of the nations, the core of the Great Commission, stands the test of time and needs no new paradigm to supplant it.

Dr. Ted Esler is the President of Missio Nexus, an association of agencies and churches representing over 30,000 Great Commission workers worldwide. After working in the computer industry, Ted became a church planter in Sarajevo, Bosnia and authored the book *Overwhelming Minority* about their family's ministry in Bosnia. In 2000, Ted became the Canadian director of Pioneers, then moved to join Pioneers USA's leadership team in 2003. Ted has BS in Computer Science and Speech Communication (Mankato State University, 1985), an MTS in Theology (Heritage Seminary, 2002), and a PhD in Intercultural Studies (Fuller Theological Seminary, 2012).

chapter 3

What's the Harm in Calling Everything Missions?[24]

by Jeff Jackson

About 15 years ago, I noticed that an increasing number of church leaders were intentionally propagating a redefinition and broadening of what *missions* is and who the word *missionary* should be applied to.

TEN CONSEQUENCES OF THE CURRENT VIEW

Though well intentioned, the view that everything is missions and every follower of Christ is a missionary comes with significant though unintended mission-impacting consequences. Here are just a few of them:

1. It causes people to gloss over the pivotal, bigger-picture facts that are clearly described in the sweep of the New Testament diminishing the attention and weight they deserve:

- Jesus commissioned His Church by way of the apostle to go and make disciples among every ethnic group, where those groups live (Matthew 28:18-20).

- The book of Acts is a record of the church's diverse but unified efforts to take Christ's commission seriously.

- The book of Revelation unveils that the commission Jesus gave will ultimately be accomplished and that He will receive worship from representatives of every ethnic and linguistic group God created. This is His end-game plan for humanity (Revelation 5:9, 7:9-10).

Because these realities provide the overarching framework in which God unfolds His ultimate plan, the understanding and motivation for every Christian to contribute is missing.

2. It provokes Christians to either ignore or reinterpret some of the key terminology that is plainly used in the New Testament:

- Jesus is referred to as an *apostle* or missionary (Hebrews 3:1).

- He gave the title *apostle* to a small and select group of His disciples called to do something that would require a unique level of sacrifice and self-denial (Luke 6:13).

- All those called *apostles* were disciples, but not all disciples were given the calling and title of *apostle*.

- The title *apostle* is applied to people other than the original 12 in the book of Acts and the rest of the New Testament, but not to all believers. The common denominator was their apparent willingness to be sent, crossing various boundaries for the sake of the gospel and the expansion of the kingdom.

- When explaining the gifts given by the Holy Spirit, Paul lists *apostle* as one of them, and then uses rhetorical questions to make the point that not every Christian is given every gift (1 Corinthians 12:27-31).

As noble and well-meaning as it is to find creative ways to encourage Christians to live out their faith and share the gospel, if God-designed diversity and distinctions—and the language used to communicate them—are blurred to accomplish that purpose, then language used to describe other areas God designed to be diverse and distinct may be more easily blurred to accomplish other apparently noble purposes.

3. It diminishes the desire to measure and know what progress has been made toward the completion of the mission He gave to His people. With that desire extinguished, the importance of becoming educated about the incredible and God-given ethnic, linguistic and cultural diversity and how it reflects His glory will be neglected.

4. It quenches the passion of God's people to pray for the remaining unengaged and unreached people groups and to plead with Him to move churches and ministries to send missionaries to live among them and share the gospel.

5. It minimizes the value and significance of advocacy within the Church on behalf of those who are still unreached and the missionaries and ministries trying to reach them.

6. It diverts financial resources away from the small group of His people God is still calling to relocate to places around the world where they will require funding from a source outside the country where they live and serve.

7. It nullifies or neutralizes the opportunities for people to participate sacrificially and financially in completing the ultimate task the Church has been given.

8. It obscures the need and thus the passion for each member to discover what they can do to partner and participate in meaningful ways with God and the missionaries He sends to complete the task.

9. It dismantles the hardwiring God has placed within us to bestow gratitude, respect and honor on those whose obedience to His calling requires an extraordinary level of self-denial, sacrifice and humility.

10. It deprives people of one of the simplest methods God has established for making the mundane meaningful—that whatever we're doing with cross-cultural missions is actually making a significant contribution towards the accomplishment of a mission that matters, especially for those who have little to no gospel access.

PROVOKING A REEXAMINATION

Although it may seem like the consequences I've listed are possible without being likely, I've encountered each of them in the churches and among the church members I interact with as part of my job.

I'm convinced this new view of missions and missionaries is harmful and hinders the completion of the mission God has given His people. So, when I encounter people who have bought into it, I point out some of the consequences listed above. If that doesn't seem to get any traction or notice, I add these points:

- We don't say every Christian who does a few of the things pastors do is a pastor.

- We don't say because every person who renders some level of medical care to others should be given the title of doctor.

- We don't say because every person in the Coast Guard knows how to swim, all of them should be called rescue swimmers.

It is very important we understand the biblical context and encourage people to share their faith. Our reasoning is easily influenced by our hyper-individualistic, extreme egalitarian culture. That culture may encourage the dangerous tendency to ignore the implications of redefining words like "mission" and "missionary." We must be very careful not to bend the meaning of words and manipulate them to mean what we want them to mean. Titles like pastors, doctors, rescue swimmer or missionary identify specific people with unique roles. If we manipulate words to mean something else, then we lose the power of their descriptive nature. Words have meaning.

Pastor Jeff Jackson served in the US Army, was a church planter in the Central Philippines and the San Diego area and pastored a church in Phoenix that was deeply engaged in ministry to the refugees who had been settled there. He currently serves as the Director of Church Relations and Missionary Care for Shepherd's Staff Mission Facilitators, a unique missions organization he founded in 2000. Jeff is married to Helen and they have three children and seven grandchildren.

Part 2:
Recalibrating Our Thinking

*Recalibrate: to calibrate (something) again. Calibrate:
1. to ascertain the caliber of (something).*
— Merriam-Webster.com

*"A weakened commitment to scripture, more than any
other factor has facilitated historical drift. It renders
us vulnerable to the subtle accommodation to culture."*
— Dr. Arnold Cook[25]

chapter 4

Missional and Missions

by Ed Stetzer

Missional has been the word of the new millennium. People, churches and mission agencies want to be missional, but where does missions fit in? If we are all missional, and everything we do is missional, how do we think about missions around the world?

DEFINING "MISSIONAL"

The terminology we use matters because terms shape the conversation we have around ideas. Terms are linguistic symbols that we develop in order to make sense of those things most significant to us. Therefore, understanding how we use terms like *missional* to describe our gospel impetus is of utmost importance for the Christian, and especially for the evangelical.

The first use of the term *missional* is over 100 years old, but how we use it today is relatively new.[26] Today, it is used to describe engagement in mission activity, a movement of like-minded churches or one's role as a missionary to his or her neighborhood. I once even heard a pastor refer to "missional lighting" in his church sanctuary.

Sometimes people also use *missional* in ways evangelicals may find problematic. Some use the term to promote social justice and societal transformation to such an extent that justice overshadows or even replaces a call to personal evangelism. Others too narrowly apply the term to refer to the call to be a missionary to one's local community or neighborhood. While this sounds admirable at first, when not seen as part of the whole, it removes focus from cross-cultural mission work. Still others use *missional* as a term to describe a different way of doing ministry that shifts the emphasis away from the program and event-based ministry popular in attractional and church-growth churches.

Missional has become an ecclesial Rorschach inkblot test. People see in it what they want, and sometimes miss what they need.

The purpose of this chapter is to help us make sure we don't lose the *missions* in the mission of God and that *missional* does not distract us from God's mission to the nations.

WHAT "MISSION" AND ITS ADJECTIVE "MISSIONAL" GET RIGHT

Despite how the term has been used differently throughout the past century and across the theological and ecclesiological spectrums, there is some common ground that can serve as a foundation of understanding. A consensus has developed over the last century and now evangelicals as well as mainline Protestants, Roman Catholics, and to some extent Orthodox Christians believe that mission is a to be more broadly understood as rooted in the identity of God and a part of the call of His people. Or, as evangelicals might put it specifically, 1) God has a mission, 2) God's mission is rooted in the identity of God Himself, and 3) God sends His people on mission.

This basis of understanding comes from the Bible, but is widely seen as being introduced (evangelicals would say re-introduced) by Karl Barth.[27] And while evangelicals would typically disagree with Barth on many other subjects, here we can agree that God has a mission and He is on mission because mission is inextricably woven into the fabric of who God is. And just as God the Father sent the Son and sent the Holy Spirit as part of His mission, so too He sends the church into the world to proclaim His gospel and raise up disciples in all nations. We see the fruit of God's mission story in John's vision in Revelation 7 where the gospel has reached every nation, tribe, people and language. It is for this purpose that God sends His people into the uttermost parts of the world to evangelize the lost.

Missional has become an ecclesial Rorscharch inkblot test. People see in it what they want, and sometimes miss what they need.

So while we can agree that God has a mission and that He is on mission, and that His mission is rooted in His own identity, and that He sends His Church on mission, I think we need more information. We need to talk about what we mean when we say *mission*. We need to talk about what we mean when we say *missional*. We need to talk about what we mean when we talk about *missio Dei*. And we need to talk about what we mean when we say *missions*, because *mission* and *missions* are not the same thing. To echo Stephen Neill's popular phrase, "If everything is mission, nothing is mission."[28] So then, what is mission? What is missional? So that we might understand what these terms mean today, it is important to first look at how mission language has evolved over time.

GETTING OUR MISSION LANGUAGE RIGHT

While it is undoubtedly true to say that mission is rooted in the identity and character of God and the church is invited to participate in the mission of God (*missio Dei*), the outworking of this idea has also been destructive to mainline Protestant conciliar mission work (think World Council of Churches). We cannot unpack the full story here, however I (and many others, more eloquently) have walked through the conciliar theology of mission and its ultimate dismantling of cross-cultural mission work.[29]

The movement that started in Edinburgh at the World Missionary Council in 1910 looked remarkably different by the 1960s, as I have written at length elsewhere.[30] And the idea of mission was the driving force for much of these changes.

Thus, it is important to understand that an idea can be both true as well as dangerous. And where things get dangerous is when the term *mission* is so broadly applied. Stephen Neill's words come back to haunt us. Neill was especially concerned about the loss of cross-cultural, traditional missions work and I share that concern today. It is among churches that consider themselves "missional" that I often find a lack of missions activity. I believe this to be for five reasons:

1. In rediscovering *missio Dei*, many have over emphasized the personal obligation to one's personal setting at the expense of the obligation to advance God's kingdom among the nations. Individualism can easily impede the global impulse.

2. In responding to *missio Dei*, many have wanted to be more mission-shaped (missional) and have therefore made everything mission (e.g. missional lighting).

3. In relating to *missio Dei*, many increasingly (and rightly) give concern to the hurting but less to the global lost. Christmas shoeboxes, global orphan projects, and ending human trafficking are all important, but they can inadvertently dim our vision for the salvation of all peoples.

4. In refocusing on *missio Dei*, many focus on gospel demonstration at the expense of gospel proclamation. One cannot read the Great Commission passages of

Jesus or the conviction of Paul without concluding the New Testament compels the Church to tell the world the good news found only in Christ.

5. In reiterating *missio Dei*, many lose sight of the Church's mandate to be a global presence with its global mission.[31]

I often hear well-meaning Christians make use of the classic Charles Spurgeon line that "every Christian is either a missionary or an imposter." If Spurgeon is right, then all believers walking with Jesus will naturally live as missionaries. But if I'm a missionary here in my neighborhood and at my grocery store—what is the man or woman selling everything they own, learning another language and moving to a foreign land to preach the gospel to a people group different from their own—often at risk of his or her own life? Surely, there is a distinction between us.

This mission about which we speak is important enough to be nuanced.

I don't intend to come down hard on Spurgeon or anyone who has reiterated his famous quote. I'm sure somewhere I'm recorded in the excitement of the moment saying it, too. But if we are going to use clarity in our terms so we can properly nuance what *mission* means, Spurgeon's quote won't do. It's simply too simplistic.

H.L. Mencken was right about this: "There is always a well-known solution to every human problem—neat, plausible, and wrong."[32] Clarity on the terminology we use is vital. Therefore, I'm of the belief that this mission about which we speak is important enough to be nuanced. We should be precise about the language we use because history has shown us that getting it wrong can have dangerous consequences.

So then what are the proper definitions of mission, missions, missional, etc.? Broadly defined we can say that *mission* is what God is doing in the world, and we join Him in it. *Missional* is simply the adjectival form of *mission*[33] and describes the mission-shaped life. *Missions* is a subset of *mission*. A more substantive way to frame it is like this:

Missio Dei: Missio Dei is *God-focused.*[34] God is on mission to glorify himself. *Missio Dei* is what God is doing in the world in light of His good character and love for His creation. This is the all-encompassing redemptive disposition of God toward His fallen creation. *Missio Dei* gives birth to the *missio ecclesiae,* the mission of the church. God is at work in the world through common grace. Through general revelation and the work of the Spirit, he is preparing hearts for him in *missio Dei.*

Mission: Mission is *everyone-focused.* This comprehensive term refers to "the entirety of the task for which the Church is sent into the world."[35] Some find it helpful to describe this mission in two complementary movements: centripetal and centrifugal.[36] The Church exhibits a quality that attracts the lost for all the right reasons. At the same time, the Church is sent into the world with a missionary purpose. Together these describe mission as something we participate in—joining in what God is doing. If you're a follower of Jesus, you're called to mission by nature of declaring Him as Lord of your life. Luke 4:18-20 describes how Jesus came to serve the hurting, the marginalized and the poor. Luke 19:10 describes how Jesus came to save the lost. Mission is this dual work of gospel proclamation and demonstration.

Missional: Missional is *believer-focused.* It describes believers and churches who live out the mission through the totality of embracing, embodying and enacting God's mission in the world.[37] Christians are being missional when, as instruments of His kingdom, they join Jesus's work of serving the hurting and saving the lost.

Note that while in the *missio Dei* God is at work through common grace, He is not at work in the world salvifically without His people. It is through His missionary agent, the Church—through that Church's proclamation—that He is at work salvifically in the world. The Church is God's Plan A for advancing His mission in the world. There is no Plan B.[38] That's part of why we need missions, with the "s" included.

The Church is God's Plan A for advancing His mission in the world. There is no Plan B.

Missions: Missions is *calling-focused*. It is the application of *mission* in a specific, usually cross-cultural response to the calling of God. So while I may engage in mission in my neighborhood, the missionary engaged in missions is responding to the call of God in a cross-cultural context. I prefer to use *missions* to refer to particular people who pursue a particular calling in a particular context. While there is a "sent-ness" in the calling of all Christians to live on mission (to be missional), missionaries are those who engage in evangelism and discipleship through cross-cultural ministry. Increasingly the interconnectedness and pluralism of our globalized world makes engagement in missions possible without leaving our own cities. These local missions opportunities will undoubtedly continue to grow. So today, serving in missions could include moving to an unreached people group in another land or moving into a predominantly Muslim community in urban America. In both cases the believer seeks to learn language, culture, and the best means to show and share Christ.

With our working definitions in order, the inevitable question is "now what?" What do we do with our language so that we might understand how to live on mission with Jesus to reach the lost? Central to our calling as followers of the King is our call to display the glory of God through the redemption of those who are far from Him.

GETTING OUR PRIORITIES STRAIGHT

If in your travels you have ever passed by another country's embassy, you may see people standing guard, usually in uniform and with their national flag. Those soldiers and the ambassador they guard inside are living, breathing representations of their own country living sent lives in a foreign land. Their task is to represent their home country and its interests while in that land.

Central to our calling as followers of the King is our call to display the glory of God through the redemption of those who are far from Him.

In 2 Corinthians 5, Paul refers to himself as an ambassador. It is an appropriate description of all Christians. The local church is, in function, an embassy of Heaven, and its people are to be ambassadors living sent lives—living, breathing representations of the King and His kingdom. As a member of a local church, you are involved in the missional task of making the invisible kingdom break through into the visible—to proclaim that the King reigns and is reconciling the world to Himself (5:19). The function of these embassies (churches) and the ambassadors within their walls (Christians) is to propagate the good news of the King and the kingdom we represent. In our case this does not simply mean that we go and do good for the city (though it includes that). It does not simply mean that we serve the poor (though it includes that, too). Paul considers a proclamation element central to our ambassadorships:

"We are ambassadors for Christ; certain that God is appealing through us. We plead on Christ's behalf, 'Be reconciled to God'" (5:20, CSB).

Justice[39] and evangelism—gospel demonstration and proclamation— are not two sides of the same coin, which implies that for one to function, the other must be hidden. Instead they are inextricably held together—the "two big rocks" of Jesus' mission: serving the hurting and saving the lost. Like a forged steel alloy created from combining carbon and iron, serving and saving forge a complete—and like the forged alloy, a stronger—witness to the world. Hiding gospel proclamation in order to foreground gospel demonstration weakens both.

While justice and evangelism go hand in hand, they must work together. Paul is careful to ask the rhetorical question "How will people hear without a preacher?" (Romans 10:14). Jesus is at work in the world, but He is not at work in the world salvifically without His Church and without gospel proclamation. This is why *missio Dei* births *missio ecclesiae,* and the Church joins Jesus on His mission to make disciples among the nations. The Church is given "the keys of the kingdom" to participate in mission with God (Matthew 16:19). The justice brought about and advocated for by the Church testifies to the goodness of the King but people must know in which King's name such good work is being done. As the Christmas hymn tells us, it is "in His name [that] all oppression shall cease."

Hiding gospel proclamation in order to foreground gospel demonstration weakens both.

I mentioned previously how, metaphorically speaking, the mission of God has two big rocks. As goes the well-known illustration, if you place a bunch of small rocks in a bucket first, the two big rocks won't fit. But if you put the big rocks in first, the small rocks fit around it. So it is with mission—the two big rocks in the mission of Jesus are serving the hurting and saving the lost: demonstration and proclamation. Countless smaller rocks surround them.

It would be reckless for us not to recognize and learn from the mistakes of those who lost *missions* in the name of *mission* just a century before us.

This helps us remember we need to prioritize gospel proclamation (which includes global missions) and gospel demonstration (also part of global mission) in the life of the Church if we would really join Jesus on His mission. The Church may do other things that are considered part of the mission, but those two things are central to the mission. They are central to the mission of the Church because they are central to the mission of Jesus. If we do not find a way to prioritize evangelism—in particular, global evangelism—we lose that emphasis.

REMEMBERING HISTORY

It would be reckless for us not to recognize and learn from the mistakes of those who lost *missions* in the name of *mission* just a century before us. Recent history sounds a warning.

The beginning of the last century was marked by the kingdom of God movement that eventually neglected gospel proclamation to become what we now call the "social gospel." It happened again following the International Missionary Conference at Willingen (1952). Mission thinkers and practitioners strayed from cross-cultural evangelism and the emphasis on church planting and favored a mission of doing good in the name of doing good rather than in the name of Jesus. H. H. Rosin notes that soon after the term *missio Dei* appeared for the first time in modern theological writing, following this conference, it began to shift in meaning from God's missionary work through the Church to God's larger work in the world.[40] Many of those who embraced this view of mission concluded that since God is at work in the world He no longer needs His Church for mission.[41] While history doesn't repeat itself, it can certainly rhyme, and we must be careful not to make similar mistakes.

How do justice and evangelism co-exist? How do we manage to accomplish both demonstration and proclamation without repeating the perilous mistakes of the *missio Dei* movement of the middle last century while also avoiding an extreme restrictivism that is all faith and no works (cf. James 2:14-26)?

How does justice not become the sole focus of the Church? I believe this lies in the prioritization of the unreached.

I am what I call an integral prioritist. I believe in integral, holistic mission—both showing and sharing the love of Jesus. We need to be doing good deeds not only because God has commanded us to but also because part of the mission of the Church is to work for the betterment of our communities. Mission is not simply making disciples who affirm disembodied doctrines. Discipleship naturally produces a faith that is vibrant and active, that is rich in good works (1 Timothy 6:18). But how does justice not become the sole focus of the Church? I believe this lies in the prioritization of the unreached.

Jesus speaks frequently of reaching the lost, of proclaiming that the kingdom has come and that the good news of the kingdom is that He invites men and women to be born again into that kingdom (see for example Matthew 20:28; Mark 1:38; Luke 4:18-21, 43; 19:10; John 3:16; 10;10; 14:6). The greatest injustice ever committed was our sinful rebellion toward God and the greatest justice God has brought to the earth He has done in Christ at the cross, making the way for all to find saving faith in Him. The parable of the lost sheep in Matthew 18 gives a clear reminder of God's prioritized desire to see lost people found. That too, should be our prioritized desire. It is from this orientation that the Church then works toward justice as a means of demonstrating here and now our certain hope of the future reign of Christ. The justice work of the Church is a foretaste of the justice brought at the return of the King.

If recent history sounds a warning, biblical history shows the way.

God's missionary purpose is seen at Babel in Genesis 9 and 11. After the flood, God told his people to scatter and multiply (Genesis 9:1). Instead, they stayed together and conspired in one language to become famous (Genesis 11). We still battle the urge to remain huddled up and to make ourselves famous. God took away man's ability to communicate with all people on the planet. In Genesis 12 through Abram God continued His mission.[42]

Between Babel and Pentecost, Israel serves as the missionary to make His name known among the nations. In the Old Testament, God's agenda was for people to come *up* to Jerusalem, as Isaiah explained, "In the last days the mountain of the LORD's house will be established at the top of the mountains and will be raised above the hills. All nations will stream to it" (Isaiah 2:2, CSB). The people of God in the Old Testament were to be on mission to bring the nations with them to Jerusalem to worship in the tongues of the nations the one true God.[43] But this mission took a dramatic turn in the Book of Acts.

When people gathered in Jerusalem at Pentecost immediately following the cross and resurrection of Jesus, something happened. Here, with a number of tribes and tongues represented (Acts 2:8-11), suddenly the message was heard in various tongues (see verse 11). Here God adds an outward thrust to His mission. When the people of God in the Old Testament did not bring the nations to God, He supernaturally brought the tongues of the people of many nations to Jerusalem for a supernatural moment. As I have written elsewhere,

> "In the Old Testament, the nations came *up* to Jerusalem. In the New Testament, Jerusalem represented a turning point for the centrifugal (outward) mission. Now, the mission of God goes *out* from Jerusalem."[44]

When we prioritize gospel proclamation, and especially global missions, we witness the fulfillment of the vision of Revelation 7:9.

> "After this I looked, and behold, a great multitude that no one could number, from every nation, from all tribes and peoples and languages, standing before the throne and before the Lamb, clothed in white robes, with palm branches in their hands."

We cannot ignore the placement of the Revelation 7:9 vision in biblical history. This passage looks to the time when the gospel has reached every remote place of the globe, compelling us to give each person on earth the opportunity to hear in their own language, "We implore you on Christ's behalf: Be reconciled to God." This vision clarifies the end and validates the means for God's missional people. The people of this vision are a resurrected people, displaying the diverse tapestry that is the people of God, living in a moment to which we all look forward—when all of creation is renewed, death is no more, and the peace and justice of Christ reign over us all. It is to that glorious end we partner on mission with God.

CONCLUSION

The history (and, honestly, demise) of conciliar missions reminds us that precision with words matters. This is especially true when considering the impact of a term like *missio Dei* and its derivative terms, *mission* and *missional*. As L.A. Hoedemaker observed, terms like *missio Dei* function like "ships carrying a broad range of cargoes."[45] These words are easily filled with a wide range of meanings that have far-reaching consequences. Once conciliar theologians and practitioners agreed that God was already on mission in the world, there was no room left for the mission of the Church.

Likewise, *missional* is a tricky term—an inkblot test. We'll see in the inkblot that which already has captivated our imaginations. Without a nuanced and biblical definition, our understanding of *missional* will reveal little more than the presuppositions we brought with us. These presuppositions, now validated by the term *missional*, can imperil the mission itself if not biblically grounded and historically informed. Our imaginations must be captivated by the arc and end of biblical history—the great story of God's salvific work through His people. Only then will *missional* and *missions* find their rightful place in the mission of God.

Ed Stetzer, Ph.D., is a professor and dean at Wheaton College where he also is executive director of the Wheaton College Billy Graham Center. He also serves as the regional director of the Lausanne Movement.

chapter 5

Acts 1:8 Sequentialism[46]

by Dr. Pam Arlund

As shocking as it may seem (at least it's shocking to me), many, many Christians are bored. They are dutiful in attending church, being good employees, raising their children, serving their communities in many wonderful and beautiful ways and yet, they are bored. How can this be? How can followers of Jesus who appear to be doing "all the right things" be bored?

I believe at least part of the problem is that they don't understand who they are. They know they belong to Jesus, but they don't understand what that means. It's true that believers are meant to attend church, build good families and serve their communities. The problem is that, although they were made for all of those things, they were also made for *more* than those things.

One of the core identities of a follower of Jesus is to be a world changer. This can be seen from the earliest days of our father Abraham when he was told that all the nations on earth would be blessed through him (Genesis 12:3). When people begin to follow Jesus, they are then joined into this family of Abraham (Galatians 3:7-9, 14). This dream of all the nations of the earth being blessed is the foundation of our faith and also the ultimate culmination of our faith (Revelation 5:9). The glory of the nations of the earth is a key building block of God's own city (Revelation 21:24-26). From these passages, it seems that *all* believers are made to be a part of God's global purposes.

One of the core identities of a follower of Jesus is to be a world changer.

Acts 1:8 helps spell out the scope of God's global glory. For many, a misunderstanding of this passage has led to a misunderstanding of who they are. Firstly, in Acts 1:8 Jesus tells us we will need the power of the Holy Spirit to be able to be witnesses of the good news of Jesus. Then, Jesus says that the gospel will go to Jerusalem, Judea and Samaria and the ends of the earth as His people serve as witnesses. Some have taken this verse to mean that the gospel will progressively move from Jerusalem then to Judea and Samaria and then the ends of the earth. Although the conjunction in this verse is far more often interpreted as "and" than "then" in the Bible, grammatical arguments are not the strongest ones to look at.

The strongest argument that this verse was *never* understood by the early Church as being sequential is the behavior of the early church itself. If the early Church had taken this verse to mean that they would *first* reach Jerusalem and then move on, then the church would likely still be in Jerusalem today. It doesn't take much of a walk around modern-day Jerusalem to realize there are many people there who are not following Jesus to this day. And, yet the early Church did finally send out a missionary team in Acts 13. There is no reason to believe that either Jerusalem or Antioch had 100% followers of Jesus at the time that the early Church sent Paul and Barnabas on their first missionary journey.

So, how did they know when to send out their first missionary teams? When the Holy Spirit told them to do so. They prayed, He spoke, they obeyed. It would have been ridiculous to argue with the Holy Spirit that Antioch had not yet been reached and therefore they could not move on to another place.

So, how is it that many believers today say, "We have so many lost here. We can't move on there until we reach all the people here." It seems to me that this statement is a fundamental misunderstanding of how the kingdom grows (or doesn't), and who we are as children of Abraham and receivers of the Holy Spirit and His gifts.

It seems that there is a deeper theological issue with saying that a particular local church is called to only local work.

Firstly, Jesus taught in the parable of the sower of the seed (Matthew 13: 1-23, 18-23, Mark 4: 1-20, Luke 8: 4-15) that only one of four kinds of soil bore any long-lasting fruit at all. This oft-quoted idea that "there are still many people here who have not been saved and so we should not move on" is the same as staying to till the poor soil. People who have heard but have not responded positively are poor soil. We are still called to love them, but the parable also calls us to move on to other soil. Jesus never implies that believers should stay and till poor soil. In fact, it seems to be a truth of the operation of the kingdom that not all will respond to the sowing of the gospel seed.

There is a deeper theological issue with saying that a particular local church is called to *only* local work. The rub is in the different gifts given to the local church. Often churches are led by someone who is a shepherd as listed in Ephesians 4. Shepherds are called to tend the flock and are usually called to a primarily local ministry. However, all who carry out the ministries in Ephesians 4 are called to equip the saints for works of service (Ephesians 4:12).

To say that a particular local body has no global calling is to decide that *no one* in that church will ever be called as an apostle. This is surely not what any local shepherd would want to imply. Local pastors understand that it is their job to "fan into flames" the gifts that the Holy Spirit has given to the members of congregation (2 Timothy 1:6). No one should condemn some gifts as not welcome within their church. To do so is poor shepherding and crushing to the hearts of those who are given an apostolic gift from Holy Spirit.

So, declaring that a local body will only reach locally denies the calling on both goers and senders.

For example, I have friends that are the first believers in a people group that has .01% believers. But, when they prayed, they felt strongly that Jesus asked them to go to another people group not their own. Logically, it might not make sense. But it's God who gifted them for global purposes and sent them out. They simply obeyed. Their own Jerusalem has almost no believers in it at all and yet they moved to "the ends of the earth," where there are also almost no believers. How did we know it was time for them to go? The same way the church in Antioch knew in Acts 13. The body prayed, Holy Spirit spoke and together we obeyed. To hold them to their own Jerusalem might have seemed logical but I am convinced that it would not have been obedience to Jesus.

I do not mean to imply that being involved in God's global glory is only for those with an apostolic gifting. For some, they will be involved by sending, for Scripture says, "How can they go unless they are sent?" (Romans 10:15) So, declaring that a local body will only reach locally denies the calling on both go-ers and senders. Often what happens is that men and women with such a gift on their lives but are in an environment that does not shepherd them in that global calling feel a lot of angst.

Globally called believers will feel torn as they try to be obe-dient to their local shepherd who only believes in local min-istry, because they are not doing what they were gifted to do. They may serve in many, many ways but they begin to slowly die inside and wonder what they are missing. In addition, if told they do not properly understand Acts 1:8, that only makes them feel worse. They wonder why they can't just settle down and do local outreach like everyone else. It's obvious that lo-cal outreach is important and something their church (like all churches) is called to do. Calling everything missions can ac-tually destroy the uniqueness of the apostolic calling. So often such people feel torn between the Spirit in them and the shep-herd they long to obey.

Calling everything missions can actually destroy the uniqueness of the apostolic calling.

As a part of this global family of God, we have joy when we are connected globally. Local bodies praying for those who do not know Jesus, giving finances, personnel and resources to the other side of the world and establishing friendships glob-ally will not weaken the church and will not damage local out-reach. In fact, calling people to global purposes and awakening them to the purpose of the family of Abraham will also awak-en people to local outreach. For the restoration of the global purpose is a repairing of the heart, even a healing of the soul of something that has been robbed of them. Not all our local church members will be goers (missionaries), but all will use their gifts in one way or another for God's global purposes and glory. Some will use their gifts of helps, intercession, baby-sitting, carpentry, etc. to achieve God's aims on a global level. Some will go out. Some will serve more locally while others serve almost exclusively cross-culturally.

Every congregation, no matter how lost the world outside its own doors is made for both local and global impact.

Let's not tell our congregants they are too insignificant and too unimportant to be connected to the global body. This is not the message of Jesus. Every congregation, no matter how lost the world outside its own doors, is made for both local and global impact. Denying one or the other is a denial of who the family of Abraham was made to be.

A people awakened to their identity in Christ will be awakened to this global identity and global belonging. To then limit their sphere of influence locally is simply not good shepherding or kingdom building. Let's call local churches to their global purpose. Let's call them to live again, to have significance, to live for more than themselves, to transform their communities and neighborhoods and to transform the whole world for Jesus.

Pam Arlund, PhD is the Global Training and Research Leader and a member of the International Leadership Team of All Nations. She previously served as a field missionary and Bible translator among an unreached people and helped ignite a movement among them. She now trains and shepherds disciples who make disciples among neglected peoples of the earth.

chapter 6

When Everything Is Missions: A Review[47]

by James Mason

"You keep using that word, I do not think it means what you think it means." Any respectable connoisseur of American film recognizes this quote from Inigo Montoya in the 1987 romantic comedy *The Princess Bride*. Throughout the movie, the Sicilian boss and hot-air artist Vizzini repeatedly describes the unfolding events as "inconceivable." Eventually Montoya, the personable swordsman, points out the obvious—when you keep using a word in so loose a fashion you eventually stop making much sense!

Much like the intelligent Montoya in *The Princess Bride*, churches today may bring to the surface a state of confusion surrounding the term *missions* and its variations. A rampant embrace of "missional" language in the Body of Christ, while helpful in some regards, has led to an unfortunate or even tragic disconnect from the biblical mandate to make disciples and plant churches cross-culturally. Words and definitions matter. Unless we are clearer about our words and definitions, we risk making the tragic mistake of missing the specificity, and by default, the priority of God's essential purpose.

If we're going to be missional, we'd better understand what God's mission is! This is an innately biblical pursuit. When we're not biblical in our broadest frame of reference, our activity boils down to personal passions rather than God's revealed purpose or direction. The many varieties of Christian activity such as personal evangelism, helping the poor and serving the local church are all biblical but are not God's central purpose. Rather, they are outcomes of His purpose, His mission. God's mission is to be known and worshipped among all peoples. This purpose is worked out through the sending of His Son who is to be declared among the nations.

The pursuit of the priority outcome often requires a long obedience in the same direction.

While all of us desire to embrace Christian ministries that pursue social transformation, true transformation is dependent on the prior existence of Christ followers in every culture. Therefore, fully equipped disciples in every nation should be the priority outcome.

In *When Everything Is Missions,* Denny Spitters states,

"To cross the barriers that missions requires, we must bring significant focus and special emphasis in the Church to making disciples resulting in churches. Without this regular and specific emphasis on 'making disciples of the nations,' the needs and outreach of the local church will always, quite naturally, receive the greatest attention of our efforts, while the voices of those with no access become a distant memory until next year's 'Missions Sunday.'"[48]

The priority outcome! This one concept alone stands in contrast to ministry activists whose mandates for action might, if we're honest, be derived from rabid passion for quick success stories and adventurism. The pursuit of *the priority outcome* often requires a long obedience in the same direction. Unfortunately, many pastors and churches find it much easier to pursue project-based strategies, both locally and cross culturally, whose benefits are far more for the success of the church and credibility of the church leaders. If we can say we're global, we're missional or we help people, then we are good pastors, good churches and good Christians. This cannot be our goal. If we are passionate about transformation, our ultimate pursuit must be the gospel within every people. When the work of missionaries has focused on *the priority outcome*—one centered in seeing obedient, worshipping communities of Jesus-followers emerge where they didn't previously exist—we see the most overall transformation. This includes economic development, health improvement, infant survival, societal justice, literacy, benefit to women and local ownership of problem solving. Truly, "making disciples who birth the local church is the key to both evangelism and social transformation."[49]

The inflated distortions of biblical mission are potentially far more devastating than the narrower specificity of making disciples in every nation. When Christians with weak concepts of missions encounter organizations or leaders who peddle equally weak frameworks the results can be detrimental. There are many examples of naïve churches giving finances to pay "native missionaries" who aren't even missionaries! Aside from the devastating dependency this creates, it also wallows in an ideology of "proxy" mission where comfortable Westerners exempt themselves from the biblical identity of being "the sent-out ones." There are numerous other examples of so-called mission activity, some of which are clearly unethical or deceiving, such as calling something global when it's clearly local. Other activities such as children's outreach or Christian radio can be applauded and supported but should not be confused with the essential task of discipling the nations. Conflating all ministries into the missions bucket leaves a massive imbalance of effort and prioritization applied toward those without any access to the knowledge of Jesus.

Above all, soul searching must include the pursuit of biblical clarity and obedience.

There is a need to pursue the critical soul searching required of thoughtful, caring and biblical Christians. This soul searching is multi-faceted. Inwardly it calls each of us to be an audience to our own motives and passions which unexamined may or may not line up with the desires and passion of God. Soul searching also includes evaluating the soul of the Church itself. We are defined by our priorities which are expressed in what we actually *do*. The church must be evaluated by its faithfulness to God's priorities and by its tenacious stand against mission drift. It is important for the Church to develop practical ways to pursue and live out a well prioritized mission vision. This could consist of the somewhat inward disciplines of prayer, repentance and reclaiming mission but they also include practical alignments with God's mission—embracing ministries such as mobilization, giving, training and organizing.

Above all, soul searching must include the pursuit of biblical clarity and obedience. One negative example of this is the "deadly sin of sequentialism" or our tendency, based on a misinterpretation of Acts 1:8, to exempt ourselves from cross-cultural or "ends of the earth" efforts. We do this, because we believe we must first focus on "our Jerusalem" and miss, or disregard that "the vision for a ministry to all nations was to be a part of all discipleship and church-planting efforts from the very beginning."[50] Instead, we must press on to a "renewed and reinvigorated commitment to the biblical, apostolic, missionary model and vision that fueled the apostle Paul, Barnabas, and Silas and that has propelled the expansion of the Church throughout the last 2,000 years—that the gospel must reach those who have never heard (Romans 15:20)."[51]

In a world of tribal knowledge and utilitarian confusion about missions, the Church must seek to embrace the conceptual and practical grounding in the beautiful essence of God's missional heart and activity. If God's perspective is shared with Christian leaders and passionate believers, it will be a meaningful contribution to the great cause of seeing God worshipped and followed in every place and people on earth.

Biblical paradigms don't come through practical utilitarian plans to fix the world; they are revealed to us in the out-workings of a God who is fulfilling His mission.

We need to thoughtfully and courageously embrace the difficult conversations that still must take place in missions. Certainly, we would all benefit from more clarity on the pros and cons of church-based sending and the role of agency partnerships in a culture that some missiologists evaluate as containing excessive and culturally bound church localism. We should also be aware of the pressure to succeed that Western churches and pastors experience. This may help relieve us from the trap that missions, however people like to define it, is often a password that gives us a distorted credibility. We should welcome these conversations and many others.

Inigo Montoya reminds us that words should mean something—particularly the word *missions*. But there is much more to consider. Christians are missing a biblical paradigm to guide our motives, our understanding and our strategies. Biblical paradigms don't come through practical utilitarian plans to fix the world; they are revealed to us in the out-workings of a God who is fulfilling His mission. Our greatest need is to be formed and molded in this paradigm. We need to be discipled. Few Christians take the time to explore in depth the idea that we have a great God, who is fulfilling a great purpose, to form a great people from among all peoples, for His ultimate glory. Maybe the Church needs to slow down its missional activism just enough to reacquaint itself with this foundational story. Once we encounter and respond to this revelation, we will be blessed, and we will be a blessing.

James Mason is on staff with Frontier Ventures in Pasadena, CA where he serves as the CEO for the Perspectives Study Program, USA, a course designed to awaken believers to pursue fulfilment of God's global purpose. After receiving a BS in education from the University of New Mexico and an MDiv from Denver Seminary, he served as a pastor for 12 years in Colorado, Kansas and Nevada. He's been married to Kelly since 1990 and they have three children.

chapter 7

The Shift from Prophet to Profit: Taking Things Too Far

by Jean Johnson

I feel a huge wave of mission drift coming over me. When I responded to the clear call of Jesus to go, make disciples, baptize and teach all that He commanded, I never would have guessed that responding to the Great Commission would translate into launching, organizing, administrating, building, fundraising and marketing. It feels like I have shifted from prophet to profit.[52]

How have I drifted so far from my original focus? Why do I spend hours upon hours creating business plans, working at the computer, hiring workers, managing people, solving problems, coordinating meetings, raising funds and tracking return on investment, yet spend little time doing what Jesus did or commanded? Why are my "Zacchaeus moments" farther and farther apart? Jesus purposefully carved out time to walk, see people, notice a "man of peace" in a tree, invite Himself to the man's home, eat a meal with him and his *oikos* and so deeply influence his life that the tax collector repented through tangible action—all without my long list of modern mission activities (Luke 19:1-9).

Have you ever had a wrestling match in your head between the tension of *profit* and *prophet* that plays out in the course of Western missions? The words profit and prophet are homophones, but have very different meanings and functions:

prof·it / präfət/ a financial gain, especially the difference between the amount earned and the amount spent in buying, operating, or producing something.[53]

proph·et / prä-fət/ Heb. nabi, from a root meaning "to bubble forth, as from a fountain," hence "to utter."[54]

Have you ever had a wrestling match in your head between the tension of profit and prophet that plays out in the course of Western missions?

Jesus designed, instructed, and modeled the essentials of missions when He mobilized and trained disciples:

"When Jesus had called the Twelve together, he gave them power and authority to drive out all demons and to cure diseases, and he sent them out to proclaim the kingdom of God and to heal the sick. He told them: "Take nothing for the journey—no staff, no bag, no bread, no money, no extra shirt. Whatever house you enter, stay there until you leave that town. If people do not welcome you, leave their town and shake the dust off your feet as a testimony against them." So they set out and went from village to village, proclaiming the good news and healing people everywhere" (Luke 9:1-6, NIV).

I see a whole lot of *prophet* and not a whole lot of *profit* in Jesus' way of approaching missions throughout the gospels. Jim Harries writes, "Jesus was a healer and a 'miracle worker,' not a project coordinator, highly trained scientist, or fundraiser."[55] We could say the same about the disciples.

Our profit-style of mission connected to our gospel doesn't translate well to many of the religions around the world.

No doubt, our Western worldview has influenced our perceived role in missions and thus our "essential activities," which has caused us to be more about profit than prophet. David Taylor, who works with the non-Western mission movement, describes our prevailing profit style of mission:

"Our natural tendency is to go to the people who are less economically privileged than we are, thus our heavy reliance on leveraging our position of economic power for the sake of mission. This is often at the expense of supernatural power and cultivating missionaries who are regarded as spiritual men and women of God by the community. Our missionaries enter cultures more like economic power-brokers than they do as mystics, faith-healers, and intercessors. Such a missionary practice is a lost art."[56]

At the end of the day, Buddhist monks and Indian gurus must look on and wonder how Christian spiritualists who come to their shores can be so wrapped up in economic affairs and power. Our profit style of mission connected to our gospel doesn't translate well to many of the religions around the world.

Scott Bessenecker, who wrote a book on freeing missions from an industrial complex, elaborates even more on how

Western culture has heavily shaped all that we have added to missions:

"Allowing ministry to be conducted by a community of 'unschooled and ordinary' people, carried along by passion for Christ and his kingdom, working together in small teams or living at the level of (and often with) the people to whom they have come, is not the story that gets central billing in the Protestant press. The colonial model crafted by a corporate ethic has left too deep an impression in Protestant mission. Few Protestant mission organizations have ventured very far from the paradigm of middle-to-upper class board members from business backgrounds guiding the mission agency with for-profit sensibilities."[57]

Jesus could have easily commanded us to go to all nations and conduct mission efforts that are all about leveraging our position of economic power through a profit system and all that comes with that. But His actual command was that we utter the Good News from a fountain of life that bubbles up and spills out on people until they either deny Him or pick up their cross and follow Him.

Jesus could have easily commanded us to go to all nations and conduct mission efforts that are all about leveraging our position of economic power through a profit system and all that comes with that.

Jesus lived His life with a prophet focus. He was in Samaria because being mobile was a strategic characteristic of a prophet. While stopping at a well, He displayed love by paying compassionate attention to a woman who had hurt herself, had been hurt by others, struggled with being bullied and lacked an authentic relationship with God. Jesus invited her to do something unacceptable by society—draw water for a Jewish man. Then He engaged in a prophetic conversation by revealing her greatest needs: healed relationships, eternal life that never runs dry and true belief. As a result, she left her heavy water jar behind and went back to her town to tell her people about the Messiah. Her life was holistically transformed.

I struggle to see much profit-style missions in the New Testament.

This story looks vastly different reimagined and spun through a modern-day lens of profit, though it may start in the same place. Jesus arrived in a town called Sychar. Feeling quite weary in the heat of the day, He sat beside a well. Strangely, a Samaritan woman walked up to the well to draw water at a time when no one would dare to do heavy chores. More strangely, Jesus asked the woman for water. This led to a conversation that revealed her heavy burdens, which were well beyond the weight of her jar. Instantly, Jesus felt compassion and started thinking about all the other women who faced hardship, brokenness and social injustices in the area.

Within a matter of weeks, Jesus launched a campaign to raise money to build Sychar's Women's Center. He asked the first woman He met at the well to serve as an employee and He promised her a salary no one in Sychar would refuse. About eight months later, He had four employees and 12 women who received economic help, easy access to water and counseling.

Jesus didn't move on to other unreached towns and villages because He had a business to run, the details of which demanded the majority of His time. Indeed, women of that village received all kinds of help and became loyal to Jesus, mainly as their patron and somewhat as their Savior. But the rest of the village was a mixed bag of responses. Some people wanted to see how they could connect and get on the payroll. Others wanted nothing to do with what looked like a prose-lytization technique preying on their poor and marginalized. Yet others could not comprehend how supposedly spiritual Jesus-people acted more like economic powerbrokers than as mystics, faith-healers and prophets.

A jarring contrast, isn't it?

I struggle to see much profit-style missions in the New Testament. Even when Jesus did something miraculous that had a high materialistic value, such as feeding 5,000 people, He did not make a habit of it, and He surely did not set up a high-maintenance project that required Him to become a chronic economic powerbroker. Instead, He quickly and sadly observed that they followed Him for His goods more so than for His Lordship (John 6:26).

Chris Little gave enlightening testimony about someone he knew on the receiving end of Western missions:

> "One day Bolacha explained to me that there are two kinds of gospels in this world. The first one, the Gospel of Christ, provides for forgiveness of sin, eternal life, and sets people free from the power of the devil. This gospel involves suffering since Christ commanded us to take up our cross and follow Him (Matthew 16:24). The second gospel, the gospel of goods...is the counterfeit gospel, which offers material wealth alongside the true Gospel, enticing people to become Christians. In his opinion, the fundamental problem with the gospel of goods is that when the goods run out the people run away."[58]

Missions that shift from prophet to profit easily confuse the nations as material goods overwhelm the message of the Good News and genuine discipleship. No matter how good our hearts and motives are, we cannot ignore our strong tendency to implement missions with an emphasis on profit over prophet.

Missions that shift from prophet to profit easily confuse the nations as material goods overwhelm the message of the Good News and genuine discipleship.

We speak endlessly about transforming the worldviews of other nations with a biblical worldview, but we have serious blind spots as to how our culture has tainted our biblical worldview and how we pass that version of Christianity on to the world. In summary, to rein in "mission as everything" to something that is more in the framework of Jesus and the gospel, we must curb our overemphasis on a profit style of missions.

Funding is fleeting, but the truth we proclaim is a treasure that "can never perish, spoil, or fade" (1 Peter 1:4). Ultimately, I suggest missionaries, mission organizations and churches evaluate their mission models and practices on an annual basis, as I have, to combat this shift. Read and pray over the Great Commission, and then take out anything that causes mission drift from Jesus' original intentions, commands and example.

Jean Johnson is Executive Director of Five Stones Global. Jean and her colleagues come alongside the global mission community to create a culture of dignity, sustainability and multiplication in Great Commission efforts. Jean has more than 34 years of cross-cultural ministry experience, which includes six years among Cambodian refugees in St. Paul/Minneapolis and 16 year in Cambodia. She is the author of *We Are Not the Hero: A Missionary's Guide to Sharing Christ, Not a Culture of Dependency* and *Go Light! Go Local! A Conscientious Approach to Short-term Missions.*

chapter 8

MissionS: Why the "S" Is Important to Church Strategy[59]

by Gary Corwin

The vocabulary that dominates the theology of mission today features a hierarchy of status describing its very essence. All the terms are derived from the Latin word *missio* (roughly translated "sent") and used to convey the concept rooted in the biblical Greek term *apostello*. At the top is *Missio Dei*. This is followed by *mission* and *missional* in the middle. Finally, at the bottom, still championed by "unsophisticated slaves to the past," is *missions*. All of which raises a couple of questions: "Are all these terms really needed? What are the distinctions that they convey?"

As to the distinctions they convey, *Missio Dei* literally means "mission of God," and includes everything that God is doing in the world to achieve His purposes. He is sovereign and all that He does in the world, either directly or through His creation agents, is part of *Missio Dei.* The part of the Missio Dei that is undertaken by Christ's Church in all of its variety is reflected in the word *mission*—the *mission* of the Church, and all it is to do in the world. *Missional* is a much more recent Anglicizing of the term to distinguish the outward or other-focus of the Church's mission from all that the Church does to teach, care for and minister to its own.

To say, for example, either that the Missio Dei and the mission of the Church is synonymous, or that the mission of the Church is all that one needs to focus on, or be concerned about, runs the very real risk of simply defining everything as mission.

While some may see it as a vestige of the colonial past, or a "from the west to the rest" approach to mission, *missions* is actually about that part of the *mission* of the Church that seeks to cross cultural, religious and ethnic boundaries to introduce and further the work of the gospel. In addition, establishing churches among those people groups and communities where Christ is least known has been distinguished over the last several decades as what *frontier missions* is all about.

As to whether all these terms are really needed, each has a particular and important emphasis, even though each may overlap or encompass at least some of what the others convey. So, they are all interrelated, but to the extent they are properly understood they each do serve a useful purpose. The problems arise when the terms are used in exclusive ways for which they are not adequate, most often in ways that directly undercut or blur the importance of the subordinate emphases.

To say, for example, either that the *Missio Dei* and the mission of the Church is synonymous, or that the mission of the church is all that one needs to focus on, or be concerned about, runs the very real risk of simply defining everything as mission. The sad history of the International Missionary Council and the World Council of Churches over the last century bears elegant testimony to this truth. The dramatic decline of their related churches in cross-cultural missionary engagement among least-reached populations has few parallels. As historian Stephen Neill once pointed out, "If everything is mission, nothing is mission."

It takes a major adjustment to our mental and spiritual orientation for us to add a focus on geographically or culturally distant people living and dying without the gospel.

Neill might have been even more correct had he said, "If everything is mission, missions is not far from extinction." The reason is that we give squeaky wheels all the attention, but even squeaky wheels that are far away are rarely heard. Human nature is very predictable regarding the setting of priorities. The things that affect us most intimately—the welfare of our family and friends, the welfare of our community and country—are always going to receive first dibs on our attention. It takes a major adjustment to our mental and spiritual orientation for us to add a focus on geographically or culturally distant people living and dying without the gospel. If people(s) and places are outside our orbit of first-hand relationships it takes a lot of information and inspiration to get us to really care. And if a missions' emphasis focusing on them is not a significant part of the burden and teaching of local churches and their members, it will almost always be ignored. Without a special emphasis on them, the needs across the street (that clearly should be addressed and have too often been neglected) will in our day tend to crowd out the needs across the world.

So rather than limiting ourselves to one or two generalized terms related to mission, or using generalized euphemisms like "outreach" instead, it really is important to be precise in what we are talking about. *Missio Dei* is about all that God does in the world. *Mission* is about all that the Church/churches do in the world. *Missional* is about what the Church/churches do to reach out beyond themselves. And *missions* is about crossing boundaries with the Gospel to minister to those with limited/least access to it. Without a special emphasis on missions, the unreached and the least reached will likely stay that way far longer than they should.

This one may not exist, but it's worth striving to emulate: It is committed to making disciples among least reached peoples and communities as the church's highest priority in missions.

An appropriate response by churches to these truths would be to ask a series of important questions: What part of the *Missio Dei* (God's work in the world) does He expect His Bride (the Church) to do? Clearly it is not to hold all things together by the power of his might (Colossians 1). That is way beyond our pay grade. But it is to be a chosen people, a holy priesthood, to reflect His glory in the world. And while the role of the churches in showing love for one another is crucial, that is not the limit of where that love needs to be shown. It needs to be missional, in reaching beyond its own in meeting human need ("loving our neighbor as ourselves"), and in declaring by life and word the glory of our God and Savior.

But even if we get all these things right, we haven't yet achieved the kind of focus that will see the gospel carried forth in obedience to the uttermost parts of the earth. The sad reality is that we human beings so easily fall into a mode of "out of sight, out of mind." And that tendency is only reinforced by the massive challenges faced by those considering labor among the least reached.

Churches, even otherwise self-identified evangelical ones, have responded to this challenge in many different ways. One might identify those responses thus:

1. We-centered churches—They don't really think about mission beyond caring for their own, and perhaps being evangelistic to the extent of adding more people to the local congregation who fit the profile of those already there.

2. Expanded We-centered churches—They don't really think about mission beyond caring for their own, but they define their own more broadly to include a mix of races, ethnicities or other distinguishing characteristics as long as the most important local church distinctives are shared. The distinctives may be theological (Pentecostal, Reformed, Mennonite, etc.), denominational (Baptist, Lutheran, Methodist, etc.), or socio-cultural (linguistic, economic, generational, etc.).

3. Missional churches—They do think about mission beyond their local congregation and are most keenly interested in impacting the larger culture of which they are a part. To some extent this is by reaching out in creative ways to other sub-cultural groups in the society, both by adding people from them to their own congregation, or by helping to establish new churches specifically geared

to reach particular groups. They tend to be largely uninterested in reaching out to those in other lands.

4. Traditional give, pray and go churches—These churches, often among the smaller ones, focus heavily, and sometimes almost exclusively, on mission work in other lands. They are happy to support the work of individuals and some agencies through finance and prayer. They are thrilled if one of their own steps forward for service overseas, but this is not common. Getting a large percentage of their congregation involved in short-term missions is not a high priority. Too often they see little or no distinction, and determine no priority, in reaching the least reached versus simply serving overseas.

5. Less traditional give, pray and go churches—More common among some of the larger congregations, these churches are more specific in their mission goals including getting many of their members involved in short-term missions; being more focused geographically, culturally or religiously in order to increase effectiveness and sustainability; and reserving at least a part of their efforts to address the needs of least-reached frontier peoples and communities.

6. Largely missionally self-sufficient mega-churches—These congregations have a clear vision (at least under their current pastoral leadership) of what their church ought to be doing in missions, and they often feel little need to work closely with agencies or other churches to achieve their goals. The particular priorities they pursue, and the accompanying agendas to achieve them, can vary widely. They may focus geographically, or emphasize short-term congregational involvement, or partnerships with overseas churches, or theological education, medical or development ministries, or church planting among least reached peoples—just to name a few possibilities.

7. The perfect church—This one may not exist, but it's worth striving to emulate: It is committed to making disciples among least-reached peoples and communities as the highest priority in missions. It understands that God's highest priority in missions is to gather "a great multitude that no one could number from every nation, from all tribes and peoples and languages, standing before the throne and before the Lamb, clothed in white robes, with palm branches in their hands, and crying out with a loud voice, 'Salvation belongs to our God who sits on the throne, and to the Lamb!'" (Revelation 7:9-10). Please note that this is the Church's and each local church's highest priority, but it is by no means all the mission and missions that churches and their individual members will be, or should be, involved in. Loving their neighbors both near and far as themselves is the horizontal half of the Great Commandment (Luke 10:27-28) that should always be reflected in how local church life and the Great Commission is pursued.

Gary R. Corwin is a missiologist, writer and editor, having served with SIM in Ghana and in various international roles for 38 years and as an editor and columnist of the Evangelical Missions Quarterly (EMQ) for 23 years. He is author/editor of By Prayer to the Nations: A Short History of SIM (Credo, 2018) and a coauthor of Introducing World Missions: A Biblical, Historical, and Practical Survey (Baker Academic, 2004, 2014). He can be reached at gary.corwin@sim.org.

Part 3:
The Challenge

"The making of definitions is in the nature of thinking. The describing of effective actions is in the nature of doing." — Ed Stetzer[60]

"Ultimately, if the church does not preach Christ and him crucified, if the church does not plant, nurture, and establish more churches, if the church does not teach the nations to obey Christ, no one else and nothing else will." — Kevin DeYoung and Greg Gilbert[61]

chapter 9

How Did the Father Send the Son?

by Jeff Lewis

What is the Great Commission? Every time I asked that question during my 32 years in missions mobilization I would receive one of two responses, Matthew 28:19-20 (most responses didn't include verse 18), or Mark 16:15. Seven years ago I challenged that popular, extra-biblical response in a chapter I wrote on the commissioning statements found in the book, *Discovering the Mission of God,* edited by Mike Barnett and Robin Martin. In that chapter I maintained that if we are serious about obeying the mission mandate of Jesus Christ, it was essential that we understood that the "Great Commission" was not a single statement but the collective whole of five statements that Jesus pronounced during the 40-day period between the resurrection and the ascension. I also argued that as we carefully listen to Jesus, we will discover the essential nuances in each statement that will guide the Church in her mission.

In Matthew 28:18-20, I focused on the imperative phrase, *make disciples of all nations,* arguing that if we are going to be faithful in carrying out that mandate then it is critical to biblically investigate how Jesus defined a disciple. Any serious study on who is a disciple of Jesus must begin with the ten scriptures in which we find Jesus using the words *matheteuo* (to disciple) or *mathetes* (a disciple): Matthew 10:24-25, 13:52, 28:19, Luke 14:26, 27, 33, John 8:31, 13:35, 15:8. It is amazing to me that we run off trying to accomplish a task we have been given without allowing Jesus to describe what a disciple looks like.

Concerning Mark 16:15, I wrote about the imperative to share the gospel of Jesus with all men, and that, similar to its use in Matthew's statement, the word "go" carries the weight of the imperative verb it precedes. In other words, to be faithful to the mandates of Jesus, His followers are to live each day strategically and intentionally in the context of the imperative statemen, "proclaim the gospel to the whole creation."

In Luke's commissioning statement, Luke 24:45-47, I used the words of Jesus to highlight the three uncompromising concepts from the Old Testament that Jesus opened the minds of the disciples to understand, concepts that must direct the life of every church and follower of Jesus. Jesus illuminated their understanding to the crucifixion and resurrection and that His message of redemption must be proclaimed to all nations. Why do we make the third statement optional in our churches?

In Acts 1:8, I concentrated on the fact that whatever God calls us to do or to be, He grants us the power and ability to accomplish it through the *dynamis* (power) of the Holy Spirit and our union with Jesus. As we live in fellowship with the triune God, we will be His faithful *martys* (witnesses, or martyrs).

That leaves John 20:21. I wish I could rewrite the chapter because I missed an essential truth about how we are to accomplish the mandates of Jesus. I now believe the tasks communicated in the above commissioning statements are built on the foundation of the commissioning statement John records for us.

A popular notion for the passage is that Jesus is emphasizing that every Christian is a missionary.

A popular notion for the passage is that Jesus is emphasizing that every Christian is a missionary. This passage does not prove that every Christian is a missionary. Not every Christian is a missionary in the same way not every Christian is a pastor. The missionary task has a specific biblical role in accomplishing the task of making disciples of all nations and planting churches where none exist. So, does that mean we have an out, an excuse not to be involved in the global mission of God? No! The biblical story clearly states that every believer is sent into the world to be strategically and intentionally engaged in the mission of God both locally and globally simultaneously. But that is another article.

John records the first post-resurrection commissioning statement Jesus announces to His followers. John also reports a similar statement that Jesus prayed four days earlier. The only variation in these two statements relates to the person or persons Jesus is speaking to. On the Thursday evening of the Last Supper and after His final instructions to His disciples, He prayed for them (and us), "As you sent me into the world, so I have sent them into the world" (John 17:18). Then on the Sunday evening of His resurrection, Jesus appeared to some of His disciples, showing them His hands and side, and commissioned them saying, "Peace be with you. As the Father has sent me, even so I am sending you" (John 20:21).

The essential question we must struggle with is "How did the Father send the Son?" How we answer this question determines whether we conclude that this statement is just another way of expressing the task we've been given in the other commissioning statements or whether this commissioning statement establishes the foundation for how we accomplish the mission of Jesus. The answer is discovered in the portrait of Jesus John paints for the reader.

The essential question we must struggle with is, "How did the Father send the Son?"

One of the central messages in John's Gospel is that Jesus is the "sent one" of God. Thirty-eight times John records Jesus confirming that He is sent by the Father.[62] The conventional approach taken to answer the question of how the Father sent the Son focuses on what Jesus was sent to do. John is clear about why the Father sent the Son. "For God did not send His Son into the world to condemn the world, but in order that the world might be saved through Him" (John 3:17). Paul affirms this in his first letter to Timothy, "The saying is trustworthy and deserving of full acceptance, that Christ Jesus came into the world to save sinners, of whom I am the foremost" (1 Timothy 1:15). The conclusion: if Jesus came to save sinners then we are sent as His ambassadors (2 Corinthians 5:20) to share the message of salvation in the world. This is true, but it doesn't explain how the Father sent the Son.

The portrait John paints of Jesus is of the Word that was not only with God, but was God, and the Word became flesh and lived in the world among us (John 1:4). Yet, Jesus does not accomplish His mission through His own self-determined effort or authority, as you would assume a god could or would do. No, John highlights that Christ the God-man lives in intimate submission to the Father. Jesus does nothing on His own initiative; He only does what the Father desires, He only says what He hears from the Father, and He only judges as the Father judges.[63] How then did the Father send the Son? As the Word of God made flesh, the One sent into the world by the Father to glorify the Father by completing the work He was sent to do, Christ accomplished His mission through daily, intimate submission to the Father's will and direction (John 1:14, 3:16-17, 17:4, 5:19-47).

The bride of Christ accomplishes the mission of God as she responds to the invitation of intimacy and walks in submission to the Father's directives.

How are we sent? We are the redeemed of God, sent into the world by the Word of God made flesh, pursuing daily intimacy with the Father, submitting to His will and direction, empowered by the Holy Spirit, so we might glorify God as we accomplish the mission He has given us. The key principle and privilege in this statement is the *daily intimate submission* to the triune God. The bride of Christ accomplishes the mission of God, making disciples of all nations, as she responds to the invitation of intimacy and walks in submission to the Father's directives.

How Jesus prays in John 17:21-23 captures this concept. In verses 17-19, He asks the Father to set His followers apart for His service as He sends them into the world. Verse 20 awakens us to the fact that Jesus was also praying for all His followers throughout the ages. Then He continues His intercession,

"... that they may all be one, just as you, Father, are in me, and I in you, that they may also be in us, so that the world

85

may believe that you have sent me. The glory that you have given me I have given to them, that they may be one even as we are one, I in them and you in me, that they may become perfectly one, so that the world may know that you sent me and loved them even as you love me."

Jesus' invitation to participate in intimacy is so the world may believe and know that the Father sent the Son.

Notice how this invitation to participate in intimacy is so the world may believe and know the Father sent the Son. This is what we have been sent into the world to do. Jesus prays that the Church would be a faithful manifestation to the world of the union and intimacy of the Father and the Son. Then Jesus invites His followers to experience the intimacy of their union. Of course, this can only happen because Christ has granted us the gift of eternal life, which He defines as knowing God and the One He has sent (John 17:2-3). Jesus then states He has given us the glory that the Father has given Him so we might live with one another in a way that expresses the intimacy of the Father-Son relationship. I would maintain the glory Jesus is referring to is the glory of the Cross, since there is no way that I will love people who are not like me unless I die to self (John 12:27-28, 17:4, Luke 14:27). I'm staggered by the thought that this is central to accomplishing His mission.

If the Son of God incarnate carried out His mission by fully relying on His heavenly Father, what makes us think such reliance is unnecessary as we seek to carry out the mission we've been given? Are we wiser than Jesus? Is it possible that we blindly go about accomplishing His mission in the wisdom of the flesh and self-effort while ignoring His commissioning prayer for us? I believe that the only hope for the church to accomplish His mission in this generation is this: We, the church, must pursue the intimacy of the Father through the knowledge of the Son and the indwelling Spirit, abiding in His Word, yielding to His daily guidance in order to make disciples of all nations. Though it may sound simplistic, should we not be still and know that He is God, and that He will be exalted among the nations and in all the earth (Psalm 46:10)? My prayer is that instead of trying to create a brand, the Church would become all that Jesus prayed for her to be, so that all nations would be discipled for the glory of His name.

For 32 years Jeff Lewis has served in missions organizations, churches, and education as a speaker and prayer leader for God's glory to the nation. sHe has ministered in 55 countries, working with field personnel and indigenous church leaders in the development of mobilization strategies, but his greatest passion is the mobilization of the church with particular focus on university students. The last 20 years he has been discipling, teaching and mobilizing at California Baptist University. Jeff has seven children and 18 grandchildren and lives in Redlands, California.

chapter 10

What Is Happening to Missionary Sending?

by Steve Beirn

Within the last decade there has been a definite upturn in creative thinking within the North American Church. This fresh thinking has birthed some wonderful new ministry initiatives and perspectives. At the same time, this creative thinking brings broader interpretations that can diminish the urgency to send missionaries.

An example of this is how the Church has floundered in its ability to generate appropriate application of Great Commission truth. Newly constructed concepts or redefined terms have altered the way the Church responds to missionary sending. These concepts have the potential to weaken missionary sending. All of us, at one time or another, have heard the statement, "you are either a missionary or a mission field," implying that every Christian is a missionary. Without clarification, this kind of thinking can move the Church away from the Biblical mandate of missionary sending.

The intent behind a statement like this is commendable. For many it has been a call to action. Yet, we have to ask ourselves, "what type of call to action?" Is this call to action the same as Romans 10:15 where the question is raised, "how are they to preach unless they are sent?"

In *When Everything is Missions,* Matthew Ellison states, "Does God expect us to pool our good ideas and pursue the things we care about or did Jesus intend to convey objective meaning and purpose when He gave His final marching orders?"[64] This informs us that we all must be careful to represent accurately the teachings of Scripture. If we don't, then we are in danger of moving in a direction never intended for the Church. The need of the hour is for all of us to fully align our definitions and concepts with the Scriptures. Otherwise, we within the Church, begin to experience unintended consequences.

The need of the hour is for all of us to fully align our definitions and concepts with the Scriptures.

Left unexplained, the phrase, "you are either a missionary or a mission field," can cause you to drift away from the greater weight of Scripture. While the Scriptures call us all to a life with a central focus of evangelism and disciple making, does that make us all missionaries? The focus on evangelism and disciple making is for us all. Yet there is a specific call or ministry assignment for some (Acts 13:2, Romans 1:1).

I have often explained it this way. All of us have a call that is selfless and obedient (2 Corinthians 5:18-20). We all attempt to respond to the broad instruction of the Scriptures. Yet, some of us have a call that is selfless, obedient and unique (Acts 13:1-3). Those experiencing a unique call with affirmation from their local church are called missionaries. They are directed by God to cross barriers of distance, language and culture to make disciples. Not everyone is directed to function like this. But all of us are directed to live out a life that is selfless and obedient. All of us can help contribute to making disciples of all the nations without that becoming our exclusive ministry assignment.

When people are told that we are all missionaries, it creates a passive posture in any personal ministry context.

Distinctions need to be made. The origin of those distinctions should come from the Scriptures. The lack of distinctions has brought on confusion and negatively impacted the commitment to send missionaries. The local church should recognize that there are many different types of ministry application when it comes to cross-cultural service. The main point is that sending should be a part of this application mix.

I have spent over 40 years in the local church. In this context, my thoughts and observations have been influenced by many things over time. My opportunity to interact with senior pastors, church staff, agency personnel, missionaries and the laity have helped me feel the pulse of the North American Church. From where I sit, I believe we are experiencing the unintended consequences of diminished sending. How does broad generic thinking like, "aren't we all missionaries?" diminish sending?

I believe there are four distinct tension points that have surfaced in the Church. To see the first tension point, we ask, "Does our theology and ministry practice challenge us to help complete the Great Commission God has given us?" When people are told that we are all missionaries, it creates a passive posture in any personal ministry context.

When people have a missionary status conferred on them, they already believe they are in their long-term ministry assignment. They stop assessing their own lives by the larger ministry context. The designation creates a large amount of inertia surrounding the remaining unfinished task. Our own theology and ministry practice should really challenge us to help complete the Great Commission. This has been God's intention all along. I have often challenged myself and others in ministry to evaluate themselves in this way.

Ask yourself, "if every local church in the world modeled itself after the ministry model of my church, would the Great Commission ever be completed?"

Ask yourself, "if every local church in the world modeled itself after the ministry model of my church, would the Great Commission ever be completed? Are our constructed concepts and definitions moving our church toward the completion of the Great Commission? Churches that have more broadly emphasized the "every Christian is a missionary" mentality have often pulled back from crossing barriers of distance, language and culture.

Some creative thinking has been born out of a desire to more fully engage the laity. It is often at the expense of a laser focus on overseas ministry. Their world of ministry has purely local boundaries. Church time, effort and resources are often used to develop the generic concept within our local church communities. This thinking has taken the local church out of God's work of making disciples of all nations. This certainly is not the case with all churches. However, my dialogue with others indicates a more widespread introduction to this mentality.

WHAT IS HAPPENING TO MISSIONARY SENDING?

The second unintended consequence is a ministry mind-set of sequential ministry based on Acts 1:8 rather than a simultaneous ministry. Some have advocated from Acts 1, that the spread of the gospel was to be a three-step process. The thinking is to concentrate effort on our Jerusalem first. When we have been effective locally, we can move to Judea and Samaria. When this ministry has largely been addressed, we go to the ends of the earth. This has created a sluggish Church. While many kinds of ethnic groups are coming to us, this is not the exclusive or even primary engagement for the Church. Every church is to express its love for the world and not just a locale.

Every church is to express its love for the world and not just a locale.

The Acts 1 text is to be interpreted simultaneously, rather than sequentially. Marv Newell in his book, *Commissioned,* explains Acts 1:8 this way, "The verse literally reads in Jerusalem *and* in all Judea *and* Samaria *and* to the ends of the earth."[65] These areas receive our time and attention simultaneously. Whatever inhibits the global focus of the Church must be evaluated. Getting more people involved in the Great Commission is an exciting thing, but it is not the task given to the Church.

The third unintended consequence of thinking that every Christian is a missionary is that it impedes strategic ministry efforts. Often the very reason people are identified as missionaries is the need to validate people and provide purpose in their present life context. This can be a commendable thing. However, when we think about strategic ministry efforts, we are thinking about action that will become catalytic toward completing the Great Commission. When we reflect on the broad thinking of every Christian a missionary, our focus and activity is almost always localized for that individual and their personal ministry surroundings.

The need is to address the ministry context where there is no gospel access.

The need is to address the ministry context where there is no gospel access. One important issue for anyone to consider is how they would define the word *strategic* in a missions context. I believe *strategic* is meeting a critical need while focusing critical influence to build the Church where it has yet to be established. From a strategic mission mindset, come helpful distinctions about the unevangelized and the unreached. The unevangelized are lost people within the sound of the gospel. The unreached are lost people not within the sound of the gospel. This distinction propels believers into a sending and going mindset. People are moved beyond their local ministry efforts.

George Murray, Chancellor of Columbia International University, has provided some definitions that make helpful distinctions. His definition of evangelism is "helping people believe in Jesus." His definition of missions is "helping people know there is a Jesus to believe in." He has often stated that evangelism is the Church growing where it is and missions is the Church going where it isn't. These distinctions help churches assess whether their focus is local, global or a balance between the two. This type of thinking helps churches remain focused on the unfinished task. Generic thinking of our day dilutes the global ministry efforts of the Church.

A final unintended consequence of "aren't we all missionaries?" is this: there is no longer a strong motivation to proactively identify and send people from within a local church body. In Acts 13 the Holy Spirit has the church leadership set apart Barnabas and Saul for cross-cultural ministry. By the laying on of hands they publicly endorsed the sending out of these two church leaders. The church at Antioch didn't wait for Barnabas and Saul to come to them. They recognized the unique opportunity to send. The more generic climate of today is not very conducive to this.

In Matthew 9:38, our Lord instructs the disciples to pray earnestly to the Lord of the harvest to send out laborers into his harvest. Some may apply this text locally and say the laborers are our "local missionaries." The question is why not also apply the text globally? The plentiful harvest is *beyond* the borders of North America. The laborers are few where the harvest is greater. The application of the text should certainly be global as well. Yet, the mindset appears to be more conducive to local ministry above anything else. The mindset is to cling to those within our church to continue to serve our local needs. We should be looking for, and developing, a Paul and Barnabas to send out to the unreached.

Are your concepts and redefined terms in alignment with God's plan for the nations?

Steve Beirn has been in local church ministry for more than 40 years. He is Global Ministries pastor at Calvary Church in Lancaster, Pennsylvania, providing leadership in mobilizing the local church to recruit, prepare, send and sustain their members in cross-cultural ministry. He received his BA in Biblical Literature at Northeastern Bible College and his MA in Ministry from Moody Graduate School. Steve and his wife, Lorraine, have three children and five grandchildren.

chapter 11

We Are Not All Missionaries, But We Are All on Mission[66]

an Interview with Dr. David Platt

EDITOR'S NOTE

Often when churches and leaders define every church ministry as missions and every disciple a missionary, we see unintended consequences. Not only do we distance our churches from the primary missions task of making disciples of all nations, we also create unhealthy missions paradigms. Denny Spitters and Matthew Ellison presented pastor and author David Platt with a series of questions to address this important issue.

Matthew: Over years of ministry you regularly speak and declare the centrality of missions to unreached and unengaged peoples as the primary missions focus of local churches. What is the foundation of your prophetic challenge to the local church?

David: Jesus' words. He has clearly commanded us not just to make disciples among as many people as possible, but to make disciples of all the nations, among all the peoples (Matthew

28:18-20; Luke 24:47). This, after all, is the ultimate purpose of God in history: to save men and women from every nation, tribe and tongue for His glory (Revelation 5; 7:9ff.). Therefore, every follower of Jesus and every leader in the church should live to see every nation reached with the gospel. If we're not focused on reaching those not yet reached, then we are either disregarding or disobeying the Great Commission.

Denny: For the past 50 years or more many believers have exited church doors and parking lots to a sign saying, "You are now entering your mission field" can you give us the good, the bad and the ugly of that phrase?

If we're not focused on reaching those not yet reached, then we are either disregarding or disobeying the Great Commission.

David: The good: we are indeed commissioned by Christ to live on mission wherever we go, and that starts wherever we live, work and play. The bad: An emphasis on "your mission field" can cause unhelpful tunnel vision such that you focus on the people/place right around you to the exclusion of people/places far beyond you. The ugly: If we all just focus on "our mission field" right around "our churches," then more than 2 billion people will continue to be born, live and die without ever hearing the gospel. We need to see the world as our mission field.

Matthew: How has the identification of every sincere viable ministry of the church "missions" and calling every disciple a "missionary," been unhelpful to global missions efforts? How might you describe or illustrate the difference between one's daily witness as His disciple to those of a missionary? Since we are all "sent" (John 20:21), isn't every believer a missionary?

David: Absolutely, every follower of Jesus has been sent, commanded and empowered to make disciples of Jesus. In this sense, we should see every facet of our lives in the context of mission. We see this all over the New Testament (arguably all over the Bible!). We are all disciple-makers on mission in the world, regardless of where we live. And even local ministry should ultimately be aimed at global mission (seeing disciples made among all the nations).

As much as I want to encourage every Christian to be on mission right where they live, if that's all we do, then thousands of people groups and billions of people will continue without even hearing the gospel.

At the same time, we also see a clear picture in a place like Acts 13 where the Holy Spirit sets apart some (not all; actually only a couple of people in the church at that time) to go where the gospel had not yet gone. Paul and Barnabas are sent out by the church specifically to proclaim the gospel and plant the Church where the gospel hadn't gone and the Church didn't exist. While the word "missionary" isn't specifically used in the Bible, I believe it's wise to call such people "missionaries." Specifically, based primarily on Acts 13:1-4, I would define a missionary as a disciple of Jesus set apart by the Holy Spirit and sent out from the church to cross geographic, cultural, and/or linguistic barriers as part of a missionary team focused on making disciples and multiplying churches among unreached peoples and places.

For this reason, I would not say, "Every Christian is a missionary." Actually, to be completely frank, I have said that before! But I wouldn't now, and here's why. I appreciate the impulse behind this statement, wanting to emphasize how every Christian is on mission to make disciples. But that's also the problem. As much as I want to encourage every Christian to be on mission right where they live, if that's all we do, then thousands of people groups and billions of people will continue without even hearing the gospel. At some point, someone has to leave where they live to proclaim the gospel and plant the Church where the gospel hasn't gone and the Church doesn't exist.

So, let's not call everybody a missionary. Yes, let's be on mission, making disciples in the power of the Spirit right where we live. At the same time, let's worship and fast and pray and ask God who He is setting apart from among us to spread the gospel among the unreached. And let's call them missionaries as we send them to the nations.

Denny: What should the priority of cross-cultural missions to unreached and unengaged peoples look like in local churches? Can every church be engaged—or does size matter?

David: By God's design, every local church not only *can* be engaged, but *must* be engaged in spreading the gospel to the unreached. This just isn't an option for any church that wants to obey the Great Commission.

The question, then, is what does this look like? Certainly, this will vary among different churches of different sizes with different factors at play. But here are a few key things every single church should do:

- Preach God's Word. Continually show God's zeal for His glory among all nations and point to how God's passion for His global glory should shape the purpose of our lives, our families, and His Church.

- Pray for the world. This, after all, is a command from Jesus (Matthew 9:35-38)—to pray for laborers to go into the harvest field. Every church should pray for un-reached people groups to be reached with the gospel and for laborers to do that work.

- Make disciples who make disciples of the nations. Biblical discipleship must always be accomplished in a global context (not disconnected from it) with a global goal (seeing disciples made among the nations). And the core competencies of disciple-making are consistent whether someone lives in the same town where they were born or among a global city where the gospel hasn't gone. As a pastor, I am working to equip every member of the church I pastor to make disciples in such a way that God could pick them up and put them anywhere in the world, and they would know how to make disciples and gather as a church in a way that more disciples could be made and more churches could be multiplied. This is a high goal, but I just don't think I as a pastor should aim for anything less.

Every church, no matter what size, can ask who God is sending out for the spread of the gospel to the unreached, and respond accordingly.

- Send laborers. Every church, no matter what size, can ask who God is sending out for the spread of the gospel to the unreached and respond accordingly. In the church I pastor, we have an Acts 13-type weekend periodically, where we fast and pray and worship, and we all lay our lives down before the Lord and we ask who He is sending out from among us. Then when I preach that Sunday, I ask people who believe the Lord may be leading them to go to stand. I've never been in a gathering where someone didn't stand.

- Participate in short-term mission trips. Much could be said about the unhealthy pictures of short-term mission trips, but there are healthy ways to utilize short-term missions for long-term impact, both around the world and in our churches. Short-term missions will often lead to long-term missionaries (and missions engagement on exponential levels).

- Give resources toward the global purpose of God. Where our treasure is, there our heart will be also (Matthew 6:21). If we want our heart to be with God's heart for the nations, then we need to put treasure here. Every church should give financial resources for the spread of God's glory among the nations.

Matthew: We all realize the significant role and influence that pastors and key leaders, elders, etc. have in leading churches in missions vision. Why do they seem reluctant to do so?

Many (maybe most) pastors and key leaders think Jesus just told us to make disciples right around us.

David: I think many pastors and key leaders aren't leading churches with missions vision (i.e., with a vision for how their local church can play a significant part in spreading the gospel to those who have never heard it) because those pastors and key leaders don't have a missions vision themselves. Many (maybe most) pastors and key leaders think Jesus just told us to make disciples right around us, and we don't have a vision for how Jesus has commanded (yes, commanded) us to work to see disciples made far from us.

Then, when pastors or key leaders do get a missions vision, they will most certainly receive pushback in the church to that vision. You look through Scripture, and you see that the people of God have always pushed against the global mission of God. So, it won't be easy. It will be costly. That means any pastor or church leader must have not only the vision of Jesus, but His courage, as well.

Denny: We often observe pastors and leaders who are confused and disconnected about the mission of the church and her central role in global missions efforts. If "Knowing comes before doing and shapes and informs the doing"—how might you encourage these pastors and leaders in their missiology and learning so they might rightly influence and lead their local fellowships?

David: There are so many things pastors and church leaders can do to grow in this area, but here are some good places to start.

- Read. Pick up a copy of John Piper's *Let the Nations Be Glad*. Read a missionary biography like *To the Golden Shore* about Adoniram Judson. Study through "God's Heart for the Nations" (a resource by Jeff Lewis available at *radical.net*). As you read, pray for your heart to be conformed to God's heart.

- Go. Spend time spreading the gospel where it hasn't yet gone. Lead the way in missions by being involved in missions. The key is: don't go where the gospel has gone. Go and spread the gospel where it hasn't yet gone.

- Come. We are about to start hosting Radical Intensives where we bring pastors and church leaders together to help one another think through how to shepherd, serve and lead the local church for global mission. Find more information at *radical.net*.

- See. Look for the relationship between local ministry and global missions. For example, when I preached last week on marriage and divorce, encouraging our members when it comes to all the challenges they're facing in marriage, I showed them the relationship between our marriages and mission. Our marriages are designed by God to display the gospel in the world. Marriage is not an end in itself. Marriage is designed by God, yes, for our good, but ultimately for His glory in the world. So, let's see this tie not just in marriage, but across every facet of the Christian life. Pastoral ministry is about shepherding disciple-makers among the nations.

Matthew: How does having a robust missions sending culture to unreached peoples impact the health of a church? Can a church be healthy and *not* engage in "Go and make disciples of all nations?"

A church will not be healthy (or biblically faithful) if it is disregarding or disobeying the Great Commission.

David: No. Simply put, a church will not be healthy (or biblically faithful) if it is disregarding or disobeying the Great Commission. And the converse is true. We can trust that when we are obeying and giving ourselves to the Great Commission (working to make disciples of all the nations), we will be a healthy church. We need not worry that obeying the Great Commission will make us an unhealthy church.

Denny: During the first 300 years of church history it seems that its structures were very nimble and organized for mission rather than being structures of command and control. How can our churches including pastors and leaders reclaim, simplify and return to a missions-centered paradigm? What needs to change?

David: I'm a bit hesitant to assume a "golden age" of sorts in the early Church, particularly when it seems from the New Testament that they had a lot of struggles from the start, and

I assume those struggles continued in subsequent centuries. I'm also hesitant to say that the most significant problems in the Church today are structural and organizational. I think more significant challenges include consumerism, materialism, unbiblical views of the church's mission, a lack of conviction about the gospel and a lack of zeal for God's glory.

Consequently, I would say that the challenge for any church leaders in any age is to serve and lead the church with zeal for God's glory among the nations, deep conviction about the gospel (including the need for Christ to be proclaimed among all peoples) and radical surrender to be and do all that Jesus calls us to be and do in this world. As we do this, we then prayerfully ask God for wisdom to know how best to organize structures to support making disciples and multiplying churches among the nations. And as God grants wisdom, we pray for courage to do all that He is calling us to do.

Dr. David Platt is the Pastor-Teacher at McLean Bible Church in McLean, Virginia. He is also the author of the bestseller *Radical: Taking Back Your Faith from the American Dream* and a 2011 follow-up book, *Radical Together: Unleashing the People of God for the Purpose of God*. His book *Something Needs to Change: A Call to Make Your Life Count in a World of Urgent Need* was published in 2019.

chapter 12

A Process of Change

by Mark Vowels

WHERE WE'VE BEEN

When I first became a member of Heritage Bible Church in Greer, South Carolina, it would be fair to say that our church held an "everything is missions" mentality. Every charitable organization of any variety to which the church made donations was listed as a "mission partner." We even partially funded pastoral interns at the church from the missions budget. There were a variety of reasons why that situation had developed.

When I was asked to oversee the missions committee, we began a process of restructuring our approach to missionary support. Frankly, that effort had gained little traction until we experienced a change in pastoral leadership. Our new senior pastor suggested a one-year missions-coaching process with Sixteen:Fifteen. This was invaluable and had two primary effects which were extremely significant.

First, it helped us sharpen our definition of missions and focus our priorities. We developed a strong vision statement:

Our aim is to proclaim Christ in order to establish reproducing, indigenous churches among the world's least reached peoples. We were also able to identify four clear objectives for our congregation:

1. Passion for God's Glory—We are driven by the character of God and the desire for peoples from all nations to join us in glorifying God and enjoying him forever.

2. Dependence in Prayer—We are empowered by the Spirit as we plead with God to save the lost and use us in that work.

3. Whole Body Engagement—Every person in our congregation has a role to play in fulfilling the Great Commission.

4. Focused Intentional Partnerships—We strategically engage with like-minded believers who labor to produce fruit in accord with our missions philosophy.

The second major accomplishment we experienced was the integration of our entire church leadership in a process of rethinking our missionary aspirations. Previously, we had unanimous perspective among our small missions committee about what our mission efforts should look like but couldn't seem to convey that perspective successfully to the larger group of elders, let alone the entire congregation. That all changed as key decision makers in our church came to the table for coaching sessions with Sixteen:Fifteen. This was a significant step which achieved buy-in and participation from all of our congregational leadership, producing ever widening ripples of influence, until we were able to confidently communicate a unified and renewed focus to the entire church family.

This process culminated in a month of sermons about missions from our pastor, a congregation-wide meeting in which past achievements were honored and future priorities were highlighted, complete with a booklet explaining the goals of the newly named HBC GO (Heritage Bible Church Global Outreach) Team. There was great enthusiasm as we explained we would be inviting engagement from all segments of the congregation to participate in what God has for us to accomplish together to expand the reach of the gospel.

WHERE WE'RE GOING

Although there are still several hurdles to cross before we more fully experience the benefits of our renewed emphasis, probably the most important one is keeping the promises that we have made for congregational engagement. Every person in our congregation has a role to play in fulfilling the Great Commission.

> **Every person in our congregation has a role to play in fulfilling the Great Commission.**

In the material distributed to the church body, we listed multiple ways to become involved in our global outreach specifically—kneel, know, give and go.

- Kneel: We created a prayer team which regularly calls everyone to pray corporately and individually for specific partners and unreached people groups. We integrate prayer for God's work in the world into our various gatherings, large and small. We need this kind of worship and consistent prayer. Prayer is the leading edge of engagement for our church's missions commitment!

- Know: Knowing comes before doing and shapes and informs the doing! We have made strategic books about missions available in our resource center and church website for awareness, education and growth. It's critical that members read and reflect on God's glorious plan to save sinners to the ends of the earth. Our Sunday morning elective hour now offers a course about missions and missionary activity around the world. We want to learn about God's global purposes and about His plans to reach the nations!

- Give: We ask everyone to give to the ongoing support of our mission partners to which our church has pledged itself. We have a Mission Partner Care Team in place and are now much better equipped to interact with and meet the needs of our mission partners, whether they are on field or home assignment. One strategic and ongoing way to give is financially, individually and as a church. We desire that people give themselves to this mission with their resources, talent, treasure and time. As our plans mature for the gospel's global advance, we hope to leverage an array of our assets as a church for the nations.

- Go: The missions committee has been expanded into a full-service Global Outreach Team. We transitioned from employing a shotgun approach—supporting random missions works around the world with minimal strategic focus—to establishing an intentional focus on fulfilling the Great Commission. The GO Team provides opportunities and funding for survey trips and educational activities intended to prepare folks who are ready to pursue missionary service. Occasionally we offer short-term trips. These are a way to get a taste of God's work in a specific part of the world. These trips help members pray effectively for and support more earnestly God's work. For some, these trips are the beginning of long-term plans to go to the nations. When their thinking about long-term missions service advances, we want to talk to them and pray about how their desires might dovetail with our missions blueprint.

WHAT'S DIFFERENT

The change process has not been easy, and it certainly has not been painless. Many things are beginning to change such as our collective approach to global missions goals as a church, how we raise global missions awareness, what and how we will fund workers, and how we disciple, identify, and send our own to the nations. It's a process requiring time, investment and patience. Let me give one example of how intentionality of mission focus began a change process.

Over the years, HBC had pledged support to dozens of missionaries, going back to the very early years of the congregation. However, we had developed a pattern of forming relationships with missionaries based upon a presentation of their vision and ministry, our church's resonance with that presentation, our potential available funding, and a vote, which produced—mission partners! We had grown this way to about 40 supported individuals, families, or ministries. While it is wonderful to support mission work around the globe and exciting to be able to say that we support a number of mission partners, it isn't practical nor best for a variety of reasons:

- The lack of strong, coherent relationship with mission partners leads to a disconnection and detachment resulting in a relationship based upon a monthly financial donation.

- We concluded we were outsourcing our responsibility to fulfill the Great Commission rather than really partnering with members of our church to accomplish our God-given call.

- Our sense of what we as a church were gifted and equipped to accomplish in global outreach was determined by other people's agendas and aspirations, rather than by our church developing and sending missionaries as an extension of our ministry.

- Rather than have dozens of loosely connected mission partners, we needed to support a number that is small enough for our entire church family to connect with and to know.

- We want to see our congregation grow in discipleship by being more actively engaged with our missionaries, and our missionaries more actively engaged with our congregation. That demands more than monthly deposits given in exchange for monthly reports.

- While we love and respect all the mission partners we have helped through the years, part of what it means to renew our focus and move forward involves restructuring our relationships with our supported missionaries gradually, generously and graciously.

WHAT'S NEXT

A key part of the plan moving forward is to prioritize missionary outcomes among peoples who are gospel destitute. The spread of the gospel among the nations is our primary ambition as a church. This has been an important shift. We want to see churches established among those who have limited or no access to the gospel. We want to see those churches led by their own people and replicating without outside help.

Finally, we are eagerly praying, researching and visiting among unreached people groups with the expectation that the Lord will make it clear to us what gospel-needy people He is calling our church to embrace. When that becomes clear, we are confident by faith that we will find our congregation to be divinely gifted with the right skills and the appropriate willingness to sacrifice for the gospel to take root among one of the world's least-reached peoples. In order to partner with God's vision for HBC we must regularly and intentionally ask of ourselves, "How are we doing—where do we go from here?"

Mark Vowels has taught missions at Bob Jones University for nearly 20 years. He also serves as director for their Center for Global Opportunities.

chapter 13

This Gospel, All Nations

by Dr. Dick Brogden

God in sovereign selection called an Iraqi and gave him a mission. Abraham was routed through Syria, sent into Egypt and plunked down in Palestine. Abraham was blessed that all nations—all the *ethne*—would be blessed in his seed.

God in sovereign wisdom decided that Moses, the law-bringer, be born and formed in Egypt, meet God and receive the law in Saudi Arabia, would marry Egyptian and Saudi brides and bring forth an Ishmaelite son.

God in sovereign mercy chose Jacob, gave him Syrian wives, called him Israel and required his family to be a light to the Gentiles. God in sovereign love caused an immigrant widow to be redeemed, mixing Moabite blood into David's veins and that the Psalms ring out hope that the nations will be glad.

God in sovereign inclusion lists four foreign women, including a Jordanian prostitute, as Jesus' ancestors and brings Romans and Lebanese into His path. God in sovereign sorrow lets a Libyan carry Christ's cross, in sovereign joy applauds Stephen's missionary sermon, and in sovereign search finds a zealot from Turkey, Paul, who will be used to bring us much of the New Testament in collaboration with Luke, a half-breed Greek.

Maybe you read these paragraphs and think, "Well I don't know, since there was no Saudi Arabia or Jordan then." Or maybe you feel that these statements are so dramatically ethnic and tribal as to be simply hyperbole. We should not discount the unique means God has chosen to bring about His redemptive plan. As we ponder the scope of God's history to redeem mankind—from the tower of Babel, to the Samaritan woman, to Revelation—let us not miss that God has always loved the nations and longs for His glory to be displayed through them.

Ultimately, God in sovereign celebration lets us know how it all ends: Every tribe, tongue, people and nation, gathered around the throne—worshipping Jesus.

The tripartite formula—dripping from every page of our missionary Bible, is that first, God is a missionary God who wants to be our God, second, our missionary God wants to live among His holy missionary people, and third, our missionary God wants to bless His missionary people for the single and priceless purpose that they bless every other peoples of earth with Jesus.

God in sovereign celebration, lets us know how it all ends: Every tribe, tongue, people and nation, gathered around the throne—worshipping Jesus.

The global population now exceeds 7 billion. Almost 42% are part of some 7,000 unreached people groups. The word "nations" in Greek, *ethne*, does not mean geopolitical states, but families, clans, cultures and ethno-linguistic peoples.

These unreached people number more than 3 billion individuals who have not heard the gospel or who have inadequate access to the message.[67]

Yes—there are lost in our decaying inner cities.

Yes—there are lost in our greedy corporate world.

Yes—there are lost in our outwardly idyllic suburb that are inwardly full of vice and depression.

Yes—there are lost on our secular campuses.

Yes, indeed our "here" is part of all the world.

But the assertion of this Matthew 24:14 text is not that the *here* is neglected but that the *there*, all the rest of the world, is at a disadvantage. We cannot join our voice to the swelling ranks of those who twist this passage and others to devote primary attention to needs at home.

But the assertion of this Matthew 24:14 text is not that the "here" is neglected but that the "there," the all the rest of the world, is at a disadvantage.

When Jesus commissioned His disciples in Acts 1:8 to be His witnesses in Jerusalem, Judea, Samaria and the ends of the earth, we must bear in mind the inconvenient truth of Acts 1:11. "Men of Galilee, why do you stand looking into heaven?" None of the disciples were from Jerusalem, none of the disciples were from Judea, none of the disciples where from Samaria and none of the disciples were from the ends of the earth! Jesus wasn't urging primary attention be devoted to home. Just the opposite. He was giving them power to leave home, leave what is safe, go into Jerusalem where your leader just died a horrible death, proclaim Christ in the power of the

Spirit, have all hell break out against you and from there keep going to the uttermost parts of the earth. The near is assumed, it is the *far* being urged. This gospel shall (must!) be preached in all the world among every people group. When it comes to allotment of resources it is always the *far* that suffer.

Imagine you are the parent of two children. Let's say your two children were both lost—both equally loved. One of them was lost in your church building and one of them lost in the Sahara Desert.

Both are lost—But they do not have equal access to being rescued. The child lost in the church complex could wander around, maybe bump into a staff member or parishioner and say. "Can you help me find my daddy?" The one lost in the Sahara could wander for 40 years and never see a living soul.

And what if—having lost both children, someone gave you a million dollars to find them, and what if you spent 970,000 dollars looking for the one lost in the church building and 30,000 dollars looking for the one lost in the Sahara? What kind of parent would you be?

Forty-two percent of the world wanders a spiritual Sahara. Christians spend next to nothing looking for them.

Forty-two percent of the world wanders a spiritual Sahara. Christians spend next to nothing looking for them.

To be clear, Jesus does not ask us to neglect the near, those wandering around lost in Christianized lands, but we must wrestle with the inequality of access. If 42% of the world is unreached, should not minimally 42% of our resources, (people, prayers and dollars) be given to the gospel of the kingdom being preached in *all* the world, to *every* unreached people group?

The word witness in Matthew 24:14 comes from the Greek word that also means "martyr," for biblically to be a witness is to be a martyr—whether by life or by death. The gospel has ever gone forth both in joy and in weeping. Men and women through the years have suffered and died for the gospel.

One of my favorite examples is a plucky Roman named Lawrence. Lawrence was martyred in Rome, August 10, 258 AD. Emperor Valerian issued an edict that all Christian leaders be put to death and their property confiscated. Sixtus II, bishop of Rome, was arrested to be executed, and deacon Lawrence called out to him as he was being led to his death:

"Will you go to heaven and leave me behind?" Sextus replied "Be comforted, you will follow me in three days."

The Roman prefect, knowing Lawrence was responsible for the church finances and thinking the church treasuries contained much gold, arrested Lawrence and demanded the church assets. Lawrence admitted the church was very rich and asked for three days to collect its treasure. Lawrence promptly dispersed the money of the church over the next three days, then gathered all the poor, widows and orphans of the congregation and on the appointed day brought them before the prefect saying: "These are the treasures of the church."

The prefect was not amused and ordered Lawrence roasted alive on a gridiron. Lawrence submitted bravely, and in the middle of his torture he said to his executioner, "You may turn me over now. I am done on this side." Then he used his last breath to pray for all the people of Rome.

A few years later in Sebaste, Armenia in 320 AD, 40 brave men further witnessed to Christ. The Edict of Milan (313 AD) mandated toleration of Christians, but Licinius, who ruled the East Roman empire while Constantine ruled the West, demanded all his legions offer sacrifices to pagan gods.

A military unit in lesser Armenia (Sivas, Turkey today) refused. They were put on the frozen pond in March, naked in the winter cold. Hot baths and fires waited them on the shores if they would recant. The 40 believers stripped themselves, marched voluntarily onto the ice singing songs and praying loudly, "Lord, we are forty who are engaged in this combat; grant that we may be forty crowned, and that no one will be wanting in this sacred number."

One of the members of the unit gave in, went to shore, was put in a hot bath and promptly died from shock. A soldier on shore watching the shivering 39 saw brilliant angels descend from heaven to crown each one. Overcome, he stripped off his clothes and ran to join the others—who were overjoyed that their prayer for 40 faithful witnesses would be answered.

The next morning the soldiers sorted through the dead, frozen bodies, putting them on a cart to be taken and burned. They found the youngest of the martyrs somehow still alive, breathing slightly. They set him aside, thinking once he revived he would recant. His mother was there. He indicated with a feeble wave of his hand that he wanted to be placed on the cart with the 39 corpses.

"Go, go my son," she cried. "Proceed to the end of this happy journey with your companions, so you will not be missing from those who present themselves before God." Then, with uncommon strength, she picked him up and put him into the wagon with his brothers.

I recently read about a brave believer in Bangladesh. He was kidnapped and asked to renounce his faith—which he refused to do. His child was brought before him and parts of his young son were cut from his body in front of the father. But the father, watching his son be progressively maimed, would not deny His Lord.

Over the last few years, many of Egypt's Coptic churches have been bombed. One young woman, widowed by the bombings, was interviewed by a Muslim television host: In the interview she forgave the attackers. The Muslim commentator was astounded. Shocked (and on national television) he admitted, "I could never forgive someone for killing my family! These Christians are made from a different substance. These Christians are made of steel."

I have concluded that the only way to die well under duress is if I die daily.

What is it about martyrs that empowers them to die singing, forgiving and smiling?

What was it in Lawrence (or the father watching his son be dismembered, the widow forgiving, or the mother who said "Go, my son!") that propelled him, while being roasted alive to address his persecutors with a grin and say: "You may turn me over now. I am done on this side?"

I'm afraid that under torture I would squeal like a stuck pig. Yet over and over again, God has graced His people with the strength to die well. I shudder to think what will happen in our time of testing, a time that draws near if we truly will engage all unreached peoples with the gospel. Will we martyr well? How will we die for the glory of Jesus? How will we witness to all peoples the matchless worth of Christ under pressure? I have concluded that the only way to die well under duress is if I die daily. If and when that fateful day comes for us, let that martyrdom, that last witness, be merely the final deposit, the last of a thousand little surrenders. Let our joy on that day come from the realization that our dying is over and our living about to begin.

I am a missionary because I want to go home. This world is not my home. I am a stranger, a pilgrim, an alien. I don't belong here. I am so weary of the filth, corruption and wickedness all around me. I am tired of death, sickness, crying, night and sin. And it's not really the sin of others out there—vile as it is—I am tired of the sin within me—the sin in my heart, the sin in my nature, the sin I return to like a dog to its vomit. I know what is within me. I know how weak, foolish, carnal, fearful, selfish, jealous, lustful and arrogant I am, and I long to be free.

I agree with Paul, who said in Philippians 1:21-23 to live is Christ but to die is gain. I don't know what will be chosen for me, but this I do know: to be with Christ is far better. We will all be changed.

"In a moment, in the twinkling of an eye, at the last trumpet. For the trumpet will sound, and the dead will be raised imperishable, and we shall be changed. For this perishable body must put on the imperishable, and this mortal body must put on immortality. When the perishable puts on the imperishable, and the mortal puts on immortality, then shall come to pass the saying that is written:

"Death is swallowed up in victory."
"O death, where is your victory?
O death, where is your sting?"

"The sting of death is sin, and the power of sin is the law. But thanks be to God, who gives us the victory through our Lord Jesus Christ" (1 Corinthians 15:52-57).

I long to go home. But the Bible clearly states we don't get to go home until we finish the task Jesus commanded of us—that disciples be made of every people group, that the gospel of the Kingdom be preached as a witness to every nation.

When I was a child, I loved Christmas—I still do. Christmas morning was my favorite. It was when we opened presents. In the weeks before Christmas we would prepare presents for one another and my parents would wrap the presents and put them under the tree. The family tradition was to open the presents early on Christmas morning. My sisters and I would rise early, eager to open the presents. If my father had said to me "And these dishes of the kitchen will be washed, all the table cleaned, as a witness, and then the end of waiting will come and we will open our presents," what do you think I would have done? I would have sprinted to the kitchen as fast as I could. I don't like doing dishes...but I love getting presents.

We have the present of eternal life waiting to be opened. When the end comes, we will have all of Jesus, our eternal gift of God. No more sin. No more curse. No more death. No more night. No more pain. No more tears; never crying again. Praises to the great I AM, we will live in the light of the risen Lamb. And all we have to do is wash the Father's dishes! All we have to do is preach the gospel of the kingdom in all the world among every people as a witness, and then the end will come. So, what are we waiting for? And how badly do we want to go home?

"And this gospel of the kingdom will be preached in all the world as a witness to all the nations, and then the end will come" (Matthew 24:14).

Dr. Dick Brogden and his wife Jennifer have served among Muslims since 1992 in Mauritania (1992), Kenya (1993-1995), Sudan (1996-2011), Egypt (2012-2018), and Saudi Arabia (2019 to present). They helped found and lead the Live Dead movement and have two beloved sons, Luke and Zack.

epilogue

Does the Church Need a ReforMission?

by Matthew Ellison & Denny Spitters

"It is our responsibility, however—our unique mission and plain priority—that this unpopular, impractical gospel message gets told, that neighbors and nations may know that Jesus is the Christ, the Son of God, and that by believing, they may have life in his name." —Kevin DeYoung and Greg Gilbert[68]

This book was designed to challenge the premise that every church activity is missions and every member is a missionary. Words have meaning, and our contributors have brought reflections on the meaning of these words bathed in their experience and insight.

History has a way of bringing clarity to the present and the future. October 2017 marked the 500th anniversary of the Protestant Reformation. On All Hallows' Eve, October 31, 1517, the Roman Church received the world's most memorable trick-or-treater when a monk named Martin Luther approached the castle church in Wittenberg, Germany and posted his 95 theses. Many Christians celebrated this historic anniversary as a time to remember the array of biblical truths the Reformation restored to the Church—*sola fide* (by faith alone), *sola scriptura* (by scripture alone), *solus Christus* (through Christ alone), *sola gratia* (by grace alone), *soli Deo gloria* (glory to God alone). Not only did the Reformation mark a rediscovery of the truth of the gospel, it enabled access to the gospel as the Bible was translated from Latin into vernacular languages across Europe.

Now, 500 years later, 7,000 people groups numbering nearly 3 billion souls have yet to hear this message that swept the world, drawing countless souls into the kingdom and transforming the face of Western civilization. These are the unreached, and they are unreached not because they are unreachable, but because we have chosen not to reach them. They are unreached because they have limited or zero access to the gospel abundance we possess!

We ask, could the ever-broadening definition of missions—regularly embraced without examination—be causing the delay in reaching and discipling these peoples who have yet to hear? Is it possible that well-intentioned attempts to expand the definition of missions have obscured the biblical priority placed on unreached peoples and obstructed efforts to see the gospel penetrate the most difficult places on earth? For many churches, missions now includes local ministry, social and economic empowerment, education and healthcare—all valid and valuable ministry. But is this the Scripture's understanding of what it means to make disciples of all nations?

As the medieval Church discovered, the gospel did not need to be redefined. It needed to be *rediscovered*. In the same way, our idea of missions need not be redefined. It merely needs to be *rediscovered*. Is this the time for a ReforMission in your church?

appendix

Churches That Changed Their Minds[69]

an interview with four church leaders

EDITOR'S NOTE

The following comes from a conversation Denny Spitters and Matthew Ellison held with a group of church mission leaders following the publication of *When Everything Is Missions*. The recording was then incorporated into a podcast of the same name. Included in the conversation were Michelle Thompson, Global Team Leader for Northville Christian Church in Danville, Indiana; Larry Hansen, Missions Pastor and Andrew Lacasse, Assistant Pastor for Calvary Murrieta in Murrieta, California; and Trent Hunter, Pastor for Preaching/Teaching for Heritage Bible Church in Greer, South Carolina.

INTRODUCTION

During the Reformation, the medieval Church found that the gospel did not need to be redefined—it needed to be rediscovered. In the same way, our idea of missions need not be redefined, it merely needs to be rediscovered. Let's hear from three churches that went through a process to rediscover missions.

Matthew: Here is a famous line from Charles Spurgeon: "Every Christian is either a missionary or an imposter." Michelle, I wonder if teaching that everyone's a missionary has ever been communicated or taught at your church?

Michelle: I would say as much as even ten or 15 years ago I did hear that. And I really think a lot of it is because people don't understand the difference between a missionary and an evangelist. Somebody who is supposed to be crossing cultural barriers or a language barrier is a missionary. An evangelist isn't necessarily crossing any cultural/language barriers.

Matthew: What do you think the motivation is for calling everyone a missionary? What's behind the idea from your perspective?

Michelle: Well, we're supposed to spread the good news. I think it elevates that sense of responsibility in people's minds. If they think of themselves as a missionary, they will maybe actually take the initiative and try to share with their friends and neighbors.

Denny: Trent, has this been an issue at all at Heritage?

Fuzzy definitions yield fuzzy execution.

Trent: I think if you go person-to-person and you asked them about what missions is, they would talk about the ends of the earth and the globe. If you were to look at our budget, you would answer it this way: "It's everything in terms of gospel advance outside the walls and immediate oversight of this church."

We had all kinds of missions partners: a local child evangelist, a regional motorcycle ministry, a camp ministry, and stateside church planting. All that was under the rubric of missions. Our situation was an example of an important insight into leadership: fuzzy definitions yield fuzzy execution. The budget, in turn, was shaping our understanding of missions. The conflict and misunderstanding we experienced in decision making as a church revealed our need for a shared definition of the task of missions.

Denny: Larry, how about at Calvary?

Larry: Many years ago, maybe 20 years ago, that philosophy was here. Currently, the majority of the folks here would not be thinking that everyone is a missionary. But it took several years for us to undo that kind of teaching and thinking. We really tried to help the folks understand that the value of being evangelistic and sharing Christ with your neighbor is the work of the Church and it is what we should be about. It's different than being sent cross-culturally. We should also be about showing the love of Christ to our friends, family and neighbors.

Matthew: Another factor here is that we've lowered our standards for what it means to be a disciple of Jesus. Feeding bellies, taking care of orphans, evangelism, is the work of every disciple at all levels in your own culture. Since that wasn't happening, we said, "Well, let's call everyone a missionary cause they'll take the job more seriously."

Trent: And thank you, folks who are out there actively doing that. We appreciate you. They're motivated and showing Christ's love in their own culture.

Matthew: That's a great comment and something we should emphasize. It's not either/or. It's both/and. It's neighbors and nations. But when you lump it all together, inevitably the nations get the short end of the stick.

Denny: Let's talk a little bit more about forces, decisions or circumstances that brought your church to a place where you recognized a need to reevaluate your understanding and definition of missions.

Michelle: We had started making a turn. When I looked at budgets from before I was involved, it was a lot of domestic campus, Christian colleges, maybe one or two foreign ministries that were in Mexico or Europe. We were coming to the realization that it was better to focus on a few and not to have our hands involved in absolutely everything. Most of our budget decisions were being made on what people's pet projects were. Our short-term mission trips were anything that made us feel good about *ourselves*. We wanted to change that.

Our short-term mission trips were anything that made us feel good about ourselves. We wanted to change that.

Trent: We kind of backed up into the question of definition. There were a number of things in our church that worked for us and at the same time worked against us. For example, generosity. Our church was founded by a group of really mission-minded saints who had an aggressive, risk-taking aim of 50% of the general budget going to global missions. It never quite got there, but while this led to some awesome sacrifices and projects, it also created a culture of watching that percentage and measuring faithfulness by it. This led to some awesome and huge sacrifices financially in sending our children to the globe. But it also led to some creativity in order to meet that requirement. We found we had a hard time explaining why we're making one decision and not another. Our difficulty was our definition of missions.

For another example, we were rich with connections. Greenville and our church are a thoroughfare for gospel work. Our desire to support those who come from or through Heritage was not sustainable. At one point we were supporting 37 separate works. Lots of connections also meant multiplying voices speaking into our church on visits about what missions is.

Even as we had some really strategic, home-grown pioneering works to be excited about, looking at the whole picture, our global efforts were many but fractured and we were fracturing relationally under the weight of it all. Getting agreement on a definition was crucial for leveraging our generosity and our connections with unity and energy for the cause of the nations.

We had heritage and legacy, but our focus was lacking.

Denny: What is God's Spirit leading us to do? What do we focus on? Churches often don't wrestle with this and assume everybody is on the same missions page. What was the missions process like at Calvary?

Andrew: I grew up at Calvary and I'm now on our missions board. I get to see things from a leadership perspective. I have seen the missions culture change. Missions was really a part of our church heritage; however, we gradually became more about the unreached and the nations. We had heritage and legacy, but our focus was lacking. We started asking some tough questions and had to kind of deal with the answers. The answers weren't always what they should be, so we moved forward with a missions vision process and then a defining process.

Denny: What were the pain points?

Larry: As we pulled our mission team together, there was confusion on definitions with just five guys in the room. We recognized that if there was some confusion between us, there definitely was confusion in the church body. What people heard first heard was that everything we had done for the last 30 years was wrong. We had to re-communicate our message to help people. We weren't saying what we had done was wrong, but that we realized that we were working in areas that were 95% reached. We had to redefine our vision, we had to talk about participation. We wanted to send the boldest, brightest and best prepared into the mission field. There definitely was a little pushback and confusion. But once we honed the message with coaching from Sixteen:Fifteen and brought it to the church it was received very well. It was a 9-12-month process before we could communicate from the pulpit. We met some resistance and decided to be very gentle with the folks who needed some encouragement to gain clarity.

Matthew: Larry, you use the word *process*. It will not happen overnight.

Denny: It's going to cost and there will be some wrestling.

Matthew: What I've realized is when you challenge the idea that not everyone's a missionary, those are fighting words and people are thrown off balance. It's a prayerful process that requires patience by saying, "Let's let our mission definitions be shaped by the Bible, not by cultural trends, preferences or prejudices, but by the God of all the nations.

Michelle: Within our team we were able to pretty quickly come to a definition that we agreed on. That was because we had gone through some studies as a team before we ever started the coaching process with Sixteen:Fifteen. It didn't take too much to get the team all on the same page. But where we really had difficulty was with our church leadership. There were places where our team wanted to clearly articulate our vision, but our elders said, "But if you make it that specific, you are going to stifle the Holy Spirit. We've got to be open to where the Holy Spirit is leading us."

Matthew: I appreciate your transparency, Michelle! I often hear folks saying "Listen, we want to be open to the Holy Spirit leading people wherever they want to go." But as they look towards the least-reached, the nations that don't have the gospel, they're afraid that they will be restricted. I often ask, "Do you mean the Holy Spirit is sending nine out of ten missionaries to places where the church has already been planted?"

We need our moorings in Scripture, and we need to allow the Bible to shape and inform our missions decisions and actions.

Trent: We invested in our process for about 18 months. It was prayerful. It was inclusive. We had our original missions committee plus key elders and deacons and a few others with missions vision. There was pain in the process. We found out how much alignment we had, but then we'd hear things like, this: "Don't we need to be focusing on local missions before we focus on global missions?" pitting those against one another. Or "Doesn't God communicate the gospel through our good works?" a nod to humanitarian work without an explicit verbal gospel witness.

We got through these conversations to settle on a shared definition of missions. Here it is: "to proclaim Christ in order to establish reproducing indigenous churches among the world's least reached peoples." Along with some value statements, this provides shared agreement for conversation in any given room regarding global missions, and adds energy to our work, especially at a core leadership level.

We need to allow the Bible to shape and inform our missions decisions and actions.

Matthew: I think a lot of churches don't take the time to develop a biblical understanding and definition of missions because their engagement in missions as a local church is really not intentional. It is reactive. They simply respond to needs and requests or outsource missions by proxy. There hasn't been a proactive vision. Churches need to have that Acts 13 season of worshipping, fasting and praying, saying, "God, we want to be a church that follows in the footsteps of this audacious church in Antioch."

What sacred cows were exposed in this process?

Larry: We reevaluated projects and people we supported to see how they line up with our values and our strategic vision. We began communicating with missionaries in the field. When we removed several from our financial support it actually went better than we hoped. The field worker had a better grasp of the church and the direction we were going. Some were very supportive, others were hurt, including church members, but having those conversations was the start to dealing with sacred cows.

We were careful to differentiate between "reached" and "unreached" and began looking for like-minded partners. We were introduced to some very unique peoples and places where we now have an established a foothold. Our pastor Brian, Andrew, and I were with one of these groups. We were able to press in with a local pastor and do some physical care, life skills and evangelism and then came back and shared the experience openly with the church body. The church immediately responded prayerfully and financially.

We were careful to differentiate between "reached" and "unreached"

Matthew: That's really good! I think without intentional, biblical and proactive vision, you end up just responding to requests and that will not lead you to an intentional action.

Trent, now that you have this biblical definition of missions that is shared, have you seen people suddenly start neglecting their neighbors and the community?

Trent: Our love for our neighbors and our desire to see the gospel grow in our immediate community is obviously where the adoption of "everyone's a missionary" comes from. It's the reason why some are hesitant about such an immersive refocusing of our global missions. But, of course, getting clear on the missionary task doesn't have to mean giving up on the local task of evangelism. In fact, they ought to feed one another. Global intentionality breeds local intentionality.

I can offer one example. After our global mission series, one young mom initiated a relationship with a manager at a local low-income housing development near our church. She's interested in ministering to single mothers in this complex and is now thinking, "If there is one thing I can do locally, I want to do this!" She's relating obedience to Christ's missions mandate to her community as a responsible Christian. We are responsible for the gospel's continued advance in our reached part of the globe. Missions intentionality and global awareness create muscle reflexes that also work locally.

Global intentionality breeds local intentionality.

Denny: At Calvary, what have you seen in this regard as the nations have been lifted up intentionally to your church body?

Andrew: Globally, we've had so many people who really want this vision. They were just waiting for us to offer them something that big and needed a channel to go through. They were so excited to be involved with that vision. A lot of people are already doing local ministry, but when we talked about the nations and focused in on unreached peoples, many people realized that there was something dire, grave and even bigger than just here in our own community.

Matthew: What do you say to the church which has an "everyone is a missionary" philosophy, but see a need to change?

Michelle: You've got a long road ahead. The transition is hard. It can be painful. It's been a long process and we're still not all the way there. There have been times I have just been ready to throw in the towel and say, "God, I am done." But every single time I've been ready to do that, God does something. I take the towel and I wipe off my brow and my tears and I say, "Okay, He is worthy. I'm not going to quit. We're going to try again. We're going to go back and we're going to scale this wall. God's got to act but we're going to do something because He is worthy."

Denny: Larry, what word of encouragement would you offer to churches that are saying everybody's a missionary?

Larry: I would encourage them to celebrate the servants among them who are actively doing something for the gospel. We want to recognize those who are actually serving, so that as you encourage them to move and change, you will build from a foundation of unity instead of a position of separation. We saw that happen and we've seen amazing and miraculous things happen due to that unity.

First, let the Word lead you and let the Word of God lead your people.

Matthew: That is a great word, Larry. For a lot of people, change is perceived as loss and suddenly they might be realizing their understanding of missions was mistaken! They may take it personally or feel slighted, so unity is vital as is encouragement.

Trent, you're a teaching pastor. Speak to other senior and teaching pastors that have a very loose understanding of missions.

Trent: First, let the Word lead you and let the Word of God lead your people. Cling to Jesus' in Luke 24 when He says, "These are my words that I spoke to you while I was still with you, that everything written about me in the Law of Moses and the Prophets and the Psalms must be fulfilled" (44). And then He opened their minds and said, "It is written, that the Christ should suffer and on the third day rise from the dead, and that repentance and forgiveness of sins should be proclaimed in His name to all nations, beginning from Jerusalem" (46, 47).

Every nation, every people is in that redemption story. Then, don't miss what's unique about our inheritance, our culture as Americans. We are a pioneering, entrepreneurial and adventurous culture, rich in education and resources. We pride ourselves in doing hard things and getting into hard places. By all means, let us leverage all of this cultural capital for the sake of the gospel. Let's get to hard places with Jesus' name with all of the risk-taking and strategic effort we can gather. Jesus' name and the nations are worth our best.

Denny: We are so encouraged to hear you say that! We often try to find our missions strategy from other churches, not the Bible. We want a quick solution, so we ape missions like "they" do it. But each church has its own unique DNA in missions. Churches don't do missions well because they don't think about missions well.

Matthew: Here are two questions for a takeaway: (1) What is God's position on missions? (2) How does He define missions? It is critical and essential to allow your church's understanding to flow out of the answer to these two questions. Thanks to each of you for sharing—we are cheering you on!

Michelle Thompson is the team leader of Northview Global at Northview Christian Church in Danville, Indiana. Because she desires for all nations to give God the glory He deserves, she works to keep missionaries on the field by providing instruction in the high school sciences for homeschooling missionary families who have few educational options for their high school students.

Larry Hansen has been a pastor for 15 years and serves as the Missions Pastor at Calvary Murrieta. His pursuit of the Great Commission and unreached peoples through mission's education, first-hand experience and partnerships combined with his strong desire for the support, equipping, and care of missionaries defines his commission of the expansion of God's kingdom.

Trent Hunter (MDiv, The Southern Baptist Theological Seminary) serves as pastor for preaching and teaching at Heritage Bible Church in Greer, South Carolina. He is a regular contributor to The Gospel Coalition and is an instructor for the Simeon Trust Workshops on Biblical Exposition. He is the author of Joshua in Crossway's Knowing the Bible series and Graphical Greek: A Quick Reference Guide for Biblical Greek. He is married to Kristi, and they have five children, Carson, Madalyn, Shae, Norah and Britton.

Andrew Lacasse is an associate pastor in Southern California working to help connect his local church to unreached peoples.

Endnotes

1. Denny Spitters and Matthew Ellison, *When Everything Is Missions* (Orlando, FL: BottomLine Media, 2017), 19.

2. Scot McKnight, "The Soul of Evangelicalism: What Will Become of Us?" *Patheos*, February 15, 2017, *https://www.patheos.com/blogs/jesuscreed/2017/02/15/soul-evangelicalism-will-become-us.*

3. Barna Group, *Translating the Great Commission: What Spreading the Gospel Means to U.S. Christians in the 21st Century* (Ventura, CA: Barna Group, 2018). 8-9.

4. David J. Hesselgrave and Ed Stetzer, eds; *MissionShift: Global Mission Issues in the Third Millennium* (Nashville, TN: B&H Publishing Group, 2010), 2.

5. A version of this chapter was published in *Mission Frontiers* 41:6 (November-December 2019), 28-31.

6. André Seumois, *Théologie Missionnaire: Délimitation de la Fonction Missionnaire de L'Eglise* (Rome: Bureau de Presse O.M.I., 1973), 9.

7. John W. Padberg, ed., *The Constitutions of the Society of Jesus and Their Complementary Norms: A Complete English Transition of the Official Latin Texts* (St. Louis, MO: The Institute of Jesuit Sources, 1996), 281.

8. David J. Bosch, *Transforming Mission: Paradigm Shifts in Theology of Mission, 20th anniversary ed.* (Maryknoll, NY: Orbis Books, 2011), 9.

9. Michael W. Stroope, *Transcending Mission: The Eclipse of a Modern Tradition* (Downers Grove, IL: IVP Academic 2017), 4.

10. Andreas J. Köstenberger, "The Place of Mission in New Testament Theology: An Attempt to Determine the Significance of Mission Within the Scope of the New Testament's Message as a Whole," *Missiology* 27:3 (July 1999), 357.

11. Of course, some will say there is no biblical word "Trinity" either. However, a major difference is that the Church has a definitive understanding of the Trinity. Any definition that differs from this orthodox statement is considered heterodoxy. The Church has no equivalent standard for missions or missionary.

12. R. Pierce Beaver, "North American Thought on the Fundamental Principles of Missions During the Twentieth Century," *Church History* 21: 4 (December 1952), 352.

13. William Ernest Hoking, *Re-Thinking Missions: A Laymen's Inquiry after One Hundred Years* (New York and London: Harper and Brothers Publishers, 1938), 19.

14. Edwin Zehner, "On the Rhetoric of Short-term Mission Appeals, with Some Practical Suggestions for Team Leaders," in Robert J. Priest, ed., *Effective Engagement in Short-Term Missions: Doing It Right* (Pasadena, CA: William Carey Library, 2008), 188.

15. Bible Exposition: Ephesians 3—John Piper (Part 2)—Cape Town 2010; accessed August 1, 2019, https://youtu.be/1a5V1O4M4rU.

16. John Stott, *Christian Mission in the Modern World* (Downers Grove, IL: InterVarsity Press, 1975), 28.

17. Robert J. Priest, "Introduction," in Robert J. Priest, ed., *Effective Engagement in Short-Term Missions: Doing It Right* (Pasadena, CA: William Carey Library, 2008), ii.

18. A. Scott Moreau, "Short-Term Missions in the Context of Missions, Inc.," in Robert J. Priest, ed., *Effective Engagement in Short-Term Missions: Doing It Right*, 16.

19. James F. Engel and William A. Dyrness, *Changing the Mind of Missions: Where Have We Gone Wrong?* (Downers Grove, IL: IVP Books, 2000).

20. Scott A. Bessenecker, *Overturning Tables: Freeing Missions from the Christian-Industrial Complex.*

21. Michael W. Stroope, *Transcending Mission: The Eclipse of a Modern Tradition* (Downers Grove, IL: IVP Academic, 2017).

22. Richard Stearns, *The Hole in Our Gospel: What Does God Expect of Us? The Answer That Changed My Life and Might Just Change the World* (Nashville, TN: Thomas Nelson, 2010).

23. Steve Addison, *The Rise and Fall of Movements: A Roadmap for Leaders* (Los Angeles: 100Movements, 2019), Kindle Location 453.

24. A version of this chapter was published in *Mission Frontiers*, 41:6 (November-December 2019), 16-17.

25. Arnold L. Cook, Historical Drift: Must My Church Die? (Chicago, IL: Moody Publishers, 2008) n.p.

26. Years ago I did a multipart series that goes much more in depth beginning with "Monday is for Missiology 3," *The Exchange with Ed Stetzer*, August 13, 2007, *https://www.christianitytoday.com/edstetzer/2007/august/monday-is-for-missiology-3.html*. See also H. H. Rosin, *'Missio Dei': An Examination of the Origin, Contents and Function of the Term in*

Protestant Missiological Discussion (Leiden: Interuniversity Institute for Missiological and Ecumenical Research, 1972).

27. John G. Flett, "A Theology of Missio Dei," *Theology in Scotland*, 2:1 (2014): 70-71.

28. Stephen Neill, *Creative Tension: The Duff Lectures* (London: Edinburgh House Press, 1959), 81.

29. E.g., *https://www.christianitytoday.com/edstetzer/2010/march/monday-is-for-missiology-how-and-why-is-god-at-work.html,* accessed July 20, 2020. For a look at the early idea of the mission of God see Georg Vicedom, *The Mission of God: An Introduction to a Theology of Mission* (trans. Gilbert A. Thiele and Dennis Hilgendorf; St. Louis: Concordia Publishing House, 1965). In German, see Georg Vicedom, *Missio Dei: Einführung in eine Theologie der Mission* (München: Chr. Kaiser Verlag, 1958). The conciliar theology of mission took a significant turn through the work of J. C. Hoekendijk. For a closer reading of Hoekendijk's mission theology, see J. C. Hoekendijk, *The Church Inside Out,* eds. L. A. Hoedemaker and Peter Tijmes, trans. Isaac C. Rottenberg (Philadelphia: Westminster Press, 1966). For a review of the origin and development of the concept "missio Dei" see Tormod Engelsviken, "Missio Dei: The Understanding and Misunderstanding of a Theological Concept in European Churches and Missiology," *International Review of Mission* 92 (2003): 481-97.

30. See for instance Ed Stetzer, "3 Historical Streams of the Missional Church Part 1: The Missionary Stream," The Exchange with Ed Stetzer, March 9, 2015, *https://www.christianitytoday.com/edstetzer/2015/march/3-historical-streams-of-missional-church-part-1-missionary-.html*; "3 Historical Streams of the Missional Church Part 2: The Missionary Stream, March 16, 2015, *https://www.christianitytoday.com/edstetzer/2015/march/3-historical-streams-of-missional-church-part-2-mission-str.html;* and "3 Historical Streams of the Missionary Church Part 3: The Missionary Stream," March

23, 2015, *https://www.christianitytoday.com/edstetzer/2015/march/3-historical-streams-of-missional-church-stream-part-3-miss.html.*

31. I've shared these reasons in multiple places, for example: Ed Stetzer, "Five Reasons Missional Churches Don't Do Global Missions—and How to Fix It," The Exchange with Ed Stetzer, September 24, 2009, *https://www.christianityto-day.com/edstetzer/2009/september/five-reasons-missional-churches-dont-do-global-missions.html.*

32. H. L. Mencken, "The Divine Afflatus," in Prejudices: Second Edition (New York: Alfred A. Knopf, 1920), 158.

33. Christopher J. H. Wright, The Mission of God: Unlocking the Bible's Grand Narrative (Downers Grove: IVP Academic, 2006), 24.

34. I am distinguishing the concept of the missio Dei from the more specific missio Dei movement in the middle of the twentieth century. See "3 Historical Streams of the Missional Church Part 3: The Missionary Stream."

35. Ed Stetzer, "Toward Missional Effeciveness: An Introduction (Part 1," The Exchange with Ed Stetzer, December 20, 2016, *https://www.christianitytoday.com/edstetzer/2016/december/towards-missional-effectiveness-introduction-part-1-of-7.html.*

36. See Johannes Blauw, The Missionary Nature of the Church: A Survey of the Biblical Theology of Mission (New York: McGraw-Hill, 1962) and Michael W. Goheen, A Light to the Nations: The Missional Church and the Biblical Story (Grand Rapids: Baker Academic, 2011), 129-32.

37. Stetzer, "Toward Missional Effectiveness."

38. Ibid.

39. "Justice" and particularly "social justice" are unfortunately politically loaded terms for many today. In this chapter, I mean by "justice" the care for those broken by sin and

marginalized by society and the work to serve them even as the gospel is proclaimed.

40. Rosin, 27-29.

41. David J. Bosch, *Transforming Mission: Paradigm Shifts in Theology of Mission* (American Society of Missiology Series 16; Maryknoll: Orbis Books, 1997), 392.

42. Ed Stetzer, "Monday Is for Missiology: Beginnings at Babel—a Thread of Hope for God's Mission, Part 2," *The Exchange with Ed Stetzer,* May 14, 2012, *https://www.christianitytoday.com/edstetzer/2012/may/monday-is-for-missiology-beginnings-at-babel--thread-of.html.*

43. Stetzer, "A Thread of Hope."

44. Ibid.

45. L. A. Hoedemaker, "The People of God and the Ends of the Earth," in *Missiology: An Ecumenical Introduction* (ed. F. J. Verstraelen et al.; Grand Rapids: Eerdmans, 1995), 164.

46. A version of this chapter was published in *Mission Frontiers,* 41:6 (November-December 2019), 18-19.

47. A version of this chapter was published in *Mission Frontiers,* 41:6 (November-December 2019), 25-26.

48. Spitters and Ellison, *When Everything Is Missions,* 48.

49. Ibid, 45.

50. Ibid, 110.

51. Ibid, 112.

52. Bessenecker, *Overturning Tables,* 67-92.

53. Google search for "profit," July 19, 2019.

54. *https://www.biblestudytools.com/dictionary/prophet.*

55. Jim Harries, *Vulnerable Mission: Insights into Christian Mission to Africa from a Position of Vulnerability* (Pasadena, CA: William Carey Library, 2011), 87.

56. David Taylor, "Missiology En Route: An Enduring Legacy," *International Journal of Frontier Missiology* 29:3 (Fall 2012), 123.

57. Bessenecker, *Overturning Tables*, 64.

58. Christopher Little, "When Two Bikes Split a Church," *Mission Frontiers,* November-December 2000, n.p.

59. This chapter is an adapted and expanded version of "MissionS: Why the "S" Is Still Important," first published in the *Evangelical Missions Quarterly* 53:2 (April 2017), 4-5.

60. Hesselgrave and Stetzer, *MissionShift*, 80.

61. Kevin DeYoung and Greg Gilbert, *What Is the Mission of the Church? Making Sense of Social Justice, Shalom, and the Great Commission* (Wheaton, IL: Crossway, 2011), 237.

62. John 3:34; 4:34; 5:23-24, 30, 36-38; 6:29, 38-39, 44, 57; 7:16, 28-29, 33; 8:16, 18, 26, 29, 42; 9:4; 10:36; 11:42; 12:44-45, 49; 13:30; 14:24; 15:21; 16:5; 17:3, 8, 18, 21, 23, 25; 20:21.

63. John 4:34, 5:19-24, 5:30, 6:38-40, 8:16-19, 38, 10:38, 12:44, 49-50, 14:3, 17:4, to list a few.

64. Spitters and Ellison, *When Everything Is Missions*, 28.

65. Marvin J. Newell, *Commissioned: What Jesus Wants You to Know as You Go* (Saint Charles, IL: Church Smart Resources, 2010), 82.

66. A version of this chapter was published in *Mission Frontiers*, 41:6 (November-December 2019), 8-11.

67. Joshua Project, *https://joshuaproject.net*.

68. DeYoung and Gilbert, *What Is the Mission of the Church?*, 249.

69. Adapted from the *When Everything Is Missions* Podcast, Season 2, Episode 2. To listen to this conversation in its entirety visit *wheneverythingismissions.com* or subscribe on iTunes.

SIXTEEN:FIFTEEN: CHURCH MISSIONS COACHING

1615.org

Sixteen:Fifteen exists to help local churches discover and use their unique gifts in partnership with others to make Christ known among all nations. They help mobilize churches to become central players in the global mission of God, unleashing them to be His channel of blessing among the nations. If you would like more information about how Sixteen:Fifteen can help unleash your church to reach the nations, please contact them at info@1615.org.

THE MISSION TABLE: MOVING CONVERSATION THAT MOVES YOU TO ACTION

missiontable.org

The Mission Table is based on the belief that a critical step in effective, church-transforming, world-changing missions mobilization is to encourage thoughtful, transparent, and stimulating conversation. This web-based video episode resource tackles the critical and controversial topics impacting missions today. The Mission Table is a resource of Sixteen:Fifteen.

PIONEERS: CHURCH PLANTING AMONG THE UNREACHED

pioneers.org

For more than 40 years, Pioneers' passion has been to see God glorified among those who are physically and spiritually isolated from the gospel of Jesus Christ. Pioneers is an international movement that partners with local churches to mobilize teams to initiate church-planting movements among unreached people groups.

WHEN EVERYTHING IS MISSIONS PODCAST

Subscribe to the When Everything Is Missions Podcast wherever you get your podcasts and listen in as Denny and Matthew, along with special guests tackle the critical and controversial topics impacting missions today.